James Lawton Thompson was born on 11th August 1936, and educated at Dean Close School, Cheltenham. He qualified as a Chartered Accountant in 1959, and did his National Service as a Second Lieutenant in the Third Royal Tank Regiment, 1959–61.

After National Service he studied at Emmanuel College, Cambridge, gaining his M.A. in 1964. In 1966 he was made a Deacon in the Church of England, and served as Curate in East Ham (London). Two years later he became Chaplain at Cuddesdon College, Oxford, and for the years 1971–78 was Rector of Thamesmead and leader of the local Ecumenical Team. In 1978 he became Bishop of Stepney.

Jim Thompson and his wife, Sally, have two teenage children, Ben and Anna. His recreations include painting, a pony and sport.

# JIM THOMPSON

# The Lord's Song

**COLLINS**
**FOUNT PAPERBACKS**

William Collins Sons & Co. Ltd
London · Glasgow · Sydney · Auckland
Toronto · Johannesburg

First published in Great Britain in 1990 by Fount Paperbacks
Fount Paperbacks is an imprint of
Collins Religious Division,
part of the Collins Publishing Group
8 Grafton Street, London W1X 3LA

Copyright © 1990 James Thompson

Printed and bound in Great Britain by
William Collins Sons & Co. Ltd, Glasgow

# CONTENTS

# INTRODUCTION

In the twenty-two years since my ordination, my family and I have only had two and a half years living outside east London. In East Ham we occupied a flat behind the door of a youth club in a highly populous area near the docks. In Thamesmead our home was a council house in a totally precast concrete environment under the shadow of tower blocks, in what was nicknamed "the town of the twenty-first century". In Stepney we spent four and a half years eight feet from the great traffic route on the Commercial Road, surrounded by impersonal buildings and more than a hint of urban decay. Now we live in Mile End, surrounded by one of our urban villages, just far enough from that other great traffic route from the east into London, the Bow Road. We have embraced the life of these urban communities and been embraced by them. We have become city dwellers, inhabitants of the complex network of roads and undergrounds, of industry and commerce, of streets and tower blocks — the whole bewildering kaleidoscope of city life. The wonderful variety of the people, the rich cultural fare, the fascination of being at the centre of the nation, contrast with the sombre realities of social and material poverty and deprivation. The need to "get back to nature" might be a cliché, but like so many clichés, there is something in it. In the midst of our city lives there has been a deep and persistent need to be close to nature. I remember once setting off with my family for a picnic from Thamesmead. I drove and drove in uncharted suburbs but we never found

anywhere to stop and picnic — certainly nowhere to light
a fire and cook our sausages. It was claustrophobic. I needed
to feel the grass under my feet, to look at the open horizon,
to sense the wildness of the animals and birds. These are
intensely ordinary things for country dwellers. So great is
the spiritual need that I have often found that twenty-four
hours in the country is an encounter with God in a way
in which I do not seem to encounter the Creator through
the cracks of our concrete city. I have come to believe that
this is not escapism, but a question of human identity —
which every fisherman knows who sits by the river for hours,
soaking up its quiet rhythm and absorbing the stillness of
God without naming the source of his re-creation.

To insulate us a little from the concrete of Thamesmead,
we were lucky enough to buy a small pony on the marshes.
We used to go and feed him in hailstorms and driving rain,
or blissful summer mornings when he was still asleep —
and we were forced to slow down to the pace of his eating
— a natural rhythm. I used to drive to the pony like a
madman, in all the urgency, anxiety and aggression of my
normal life — and after three-quarters of an hour in his
quiet company, I would drive home as relaxed as though
in a horse and cart from a quieter, more spacious age.

I am sure I am not alone in feeling a tension between
the bustling and often exciting world of the city and the
deep rhythms of nature. The combination and the tension
between the two deepen our perception of what human life
could be. It is in part the memory of the meadows and the
mountains that makes me angry when I see disgusting,
crowded flats and smelly lifts and staircases — it is in part
the vividness and intricacy of nature which makes me long

for an end to vandalism against the spirit and soul of the city dwellers who have no say against it, whether it is the violence of an alienated heart or the planner's drawing board. Spending time in a village makes me want to fight against the isolation and anonymity of the spy-hole city. On the other hand, when I realize the narrowness of some rural life, the cruelty which a village's lack of privacy brings and the persistent cruelty of nature herself, I can sometimes appreciate the security and anonymity of the city.

This is a proper tension with which we have to live. I have found in my prayers that nothing comforts me so much as praying the psalms in the city. I must confess that some of the psalms leave me as yet unmoved, but others have become the heartbeat of my own struggling prayer. I am not a scholar, as will be immediately apparent to any reader who knows a little, and this book would be of little use to professional theologians who must turn every stone. I have simply made a choice of the psalms that mean a lot to me, in the hope that I may share their strength. It is my hope that those readers who are not yet converts to the psalms might develop a taste for them and want to tackle the other 140 for themselves. For those who know them well, maybe this little book can be a stimulus to further thought and prayer.

For me, the experience of reading, praying or singing a psalm is rather like looking at a painting or listening to a piece of music. There is the immediate impact of its beauty, its truth and its harmony directly enjoyed. But there are other layers of perception. For instance, what did the painter or composer intend to say? This can often best be understood by getting inside the setting in whcih they lived.

The music and the paintings were created by individual people at a particular moment in history, individual people with all their own fears and hopes, their laughter and their tears. So I can hear the psalmist speaking to me more clearly if I can get inside his experience and see what he saw, and feel what he felt. To understand a little of what it means to be exiled makes Psalm 137 come alive:

> By the waters of Babylon we sat down and wept:
> when we remembered Zion.
>
> (PSALM 137:1)

To experience persecution for faith sharpens up our sharing in Psalm 22:

> My hands and feet are withered:
> and you lay me in the dust of death.
> For many dogs are come about me:
> and a band of evildoers hem me in.
>
> (PSALM 22:16–17)

If you look at the music of a soloist's song sheet, you may imagine an individual singing of his love or of a legend, whereas the music of a great choral composition may conjure up the cathedral, the massed choir, the orchestra and all the people sharing in the glory of it all. In the same way, the psalms are sometimes the quiet prayer or meditation of an individual:

> My soul waits in silence for God:
> for from him comes my salvation.
> He only is my rock and my salvation:
> my strong tower so that I shall never be moved.
>
> (PSALM 62:1–2)

10

and sometimes the expression of the corporate worship in
the temple:

> Lift up your heads O you gates
> and be lifted up you everlasting doors:
> and the King of glory shall come in.
> Who is the King of glory?
> the Lord of hosts he is the King of glory.
>
> (PSALM 24:9–10)

They sometimes express the most intimate feelings of an
individual in his pilgrimage:

> Nevertheless my feet were almost gone:
> my steps had well-nigh slipped.
> For I was filled with envy at the boastful
> when I saw the ungodly had such tranquillity.
>
> (PSALM 73:2–3)

and sometimes trumpet the whole splendour of God's
wonderful majesty:

> Praise the Lord.
> Praise the Lord from heaven:
> O praise him in the heights.
> Praise him all his angels:
> O praise him all his host.
> Praise him sun and moon:
> praise him all you stars of light.
> Praise him you highest heaven:
> and you waters that are above the heavens.
>
> (PSALM 148:1–4)

They sometimes recall the sacred history of the people of Israel:

> At Horeb they made themselves a calf:
> and bowed down in wander to an image.
> And so they exchanged the glory of God:
> for the likeness of an ox that eats hay.
> They forgot God who was their saviour:
> that had done such great things in Egypt.
>
> (PSALM 106:20-22)

And sometimes speak the universal word to mankind:

> For you have created my inward parts:
> you knit me together in my mother's womb.
> I will praise you for you are to be feared:
> fearful are your acts and wonderful your works.
>
> (PSALM 139:12-13)

When we think of someone praying, we often conjure up a picture of a person very still, with eyes closed, perhaps with hands together, pointing to heaven. It all looks very controlled, and our worship in church looks very calm and respectable. When we use the psalms in worship, the passion, the anger, the joy, the fear, the faith of the psalmist seem worlds away from the muted, inhibited prayer of our churches. The prayer of the psalmists – like the prayer of Jesus – is a body and soul activity involving every emotion, vivid, passionate, urgent and issuing from the whole experience of the human being and the human race. The prayers of Jesus have a totally down-to-earth sound:

> My heart is ready to break with grief.
>
> (MATTHEW 26:38)

My Father, if it is possible, let this cup pass me by.

(MATTHEW 26:39)

There is nothing in human experience which the psalmists do not send to God in prayer. This can be very uncomfortable − not just because it does not seem very respectable to feel things so deeply, but also because when we recite them, we find ourselves using words of hate and the desire for another's destruction. Perhaps those prayers would be more acceptable to us if our homes had been destroyed, our family tortured and killed, our children abused. But this hating side of the psalms is a real difficulty, and liturgically Churches have tried to omit the bits which are sub-Christian in their experience:

> Break their teeth O God in their mouths:
> shatter the jaws of the young lions O Lord.
> Let them dissolve and drain away like water:
> let them be trodden down, let them wither
>    like grass.

(PSALM 58:6−7)

Whilst I accept that these and similar passages are not helpful in worship, they are a solemn reminder of the nature of the human being − who is capable of sublime affection and philosophy, and yet is able to hate. Prayer has to reach into the hard, angry places of the heart. The depth of the psalms is in part drawn from their expression of our whole human struggle, our search for identity and our search for God. There is none of the pale anaemic religion in these whole offerings of man's whole being to God:

> Shout for joy before the Lord, you who are righteous.

(PSALM 33:1, NEB)

13

My soul is thirsty for God, thirsty for the
  living God:
when shall I come and see his face?
My tears have been my food day and night:
while they ask me all day long, "Where now
  is your God?"

(PSALM 42:2-3)

Why hast thou cast us off, O God?
Is it for ever?

(PSALM 74:1, NEB)

O God to whom vengeance belongs, shine out
  in glory.
Arise, judge of the earth:
and requite the proud as they deserve.
Lord, how long shall the wicked:
how long shall the wicked triumph?
How long shall all evildoers pour out words:
how long shall they boast and flaunt themselves?
They crush your people, O Lord:
they oppress your own possession.
They murder the widow and the alien:
they put the fatherless to death.

(PSALM 94:1-6)

My God, my God, why have you forsaken me:
why are you so far from helping me
and from the words of my groaning?

(PSALM 22:1)

Every emotion and every experience – birth, death,
isolation, panic, envy, anger, wonder, joy, peace and conflict,

14

war, oppression, slavery, the happiness of more peaceful times and the beauty of the Temple, the moment of pure stillness before God and the ecstasy of the vast congregation – all are there.

So we try to enter into the psalmist's experience and his own setting, to discover and share his faith, his struggle and his hope. From understanding his context, we can move on to encounter God in our own day and our own setting, in our own hearts and minds, and in our own worship. In many ways it is a help to have a reflection of ourselves in another age, to look through the eyes of the pilgrim then, to put our own pilgrimage here and now into perspective and sometimes be shocked out of our habits of thought – our narrow contemporary way of seeing reality.

In the end, we are looking for a way of walking in our own daily lives. Our twentieth-century western Europe has, through all our sophistication, our demythologizing, our absurd claims, our materialistic understanding, deprived us of our capacity for a proper sense of mystery and all but closed the gate of heaven, so that we find it difficult to glimpse the eternal. The void of a funeral without any faith, the ruthless exploitation of the beautiful earth, the brutalization and banality of our social milieu, the pathetic dis-eases in our personal relationships, all ought to humble us to look towards our universe – not with the self-confidence of man come of age, with the assurance that human progress is inevitable if only man will make rational decisions – but rather with humility and awe, only too aware of how prone we are to hurt and to destroy.

To encounter and use the psalms over a long period of time means to give ourselves an eternal language, to find a way of walking with God, of facing reality red in tooth and claw, and finding the faith and the hope to go on. When we get inside them we can never indulge in that escapism which keeps our spiritual life separate from the mainstream of political and social and personal struggle. The spiritual life we discover in the psalms is one which slowly becomes part of our whole way – affecting both our private and our public life, our individual and our corporate concerns. This book is in no way comprehensive. It has been written in the middle of all my own particular battles here in East London. It may be a little frayed at the edges, and it is certainly far from impartial, because it bears the scars of all the disappointments, hurt and defeats of my own experience, as well as the encouragement of the many beauties of people and of God as He and they are encountered. I have felt a tremendous need to explore a way of prayer which grows out of trying to be a contemporary person. As I leave my quiet time to travel in a tube train packed like a cattle truck, to go back into all the complexities and turmoil of a city life, I long to keep a sense of God who guides, strengthens and inspires my life in the teeming world.

The psalms are a springboard for prayer, meditation and worship. I shall try to begin from their original meaning in their original setting but, just as our prayers cannot be fastened down, so I will take off, and hope that readers will find themselves travelling from the rivers of Babylon to the River Thames. I have been encouraged in this freedom by St Augustine's great exposition of the Psalms. He constantly goes into orbit, and is almost writing new Christian psalms as he springs from thought to thought. I do not find his use of allegory always helpful. In Psalm 104, for instance, the whole purpose of the psalm seems to be lost and distorted by his determination to find a meaning tied to Christ, the Church, the apostles, in every line, behind every cloud, wind and mountain. Such allegories do not seem to work for us because they do violence to what was originally written. But allegories were all the rage in Augustine's day, and we have to remember that he believed – as indeed Christians do in our day – that Christ, the Word, was the source of all the words of God. He was not trying so much to give an accurate, word-for-word account of the psalms, as to use them to stir and move and chasten and encourage his readers to find in their prayers their Lord and Master:

> Come, my brethren, catch my eagerness; share with me in this my longing: let us both love, let us both be inflamed with this thirst, let us both hasten to the well of understanding.[1]

Augustine was not restricted or stimulated by modern studies. He had no modern translation, nor many centuries of further theological reflection. He trusted that the psalms would help him to lead others closer to God, and that was what he wanted: 'Better is it that scholars find fault with us, than that the people understand us not.'[2]

I have written this book in company with several commentators. Although St Augustine towers above us all, I have also come to appreciate many of our contemporary theologians, who respect the integrity of the text and take us back so skilfully to its original setting. In the end, our highest ambition is that we shall be able to sing the Lord's song in our own time and place, from our own soul.

Before turning to the text, there is one more important fact which we must remember about the background to the psalms – a layer of perception which we must recognize. The psalms are the spiritual heritage of the Jews, as they were of the Jew, Jesus. In their composition they are pre-Christian, though Christians through two thousand years have used them and prayed them as a mainstream of their worship of God. In the Christian Church, we finish the reading of each psalm with the praise to God as understood through Christ's eyes:

> Glory be to the Father, and to the Son,
> and to the Holy Spirit:
> as it was in the beginning, is now,
> and shall be for ever. Amen.

In a sense, this reminds us that it is our belief that the yearning of the Old Testament was fulfilled in the life of Jesus. The phrase which appears most often in the English text as "the Lord" points sharply to the difference between the Jewish and the Christian readers of the psalms. For the Jews, "the Lord" in Hebrew is the word *Adonai* – used by the Jew to avoid using the name of God and so breeding familiarity with Him. When the phrase was translated into Greek, it became *kurios* – "the Lord", and the Christians' experience made them say, "Jesus is Lord". So the Christian brings to the praying of the psalms the belief, the layer of perception, which Jesus claimed: "He that has seen me has seen the Father." We therefore look for consistency with what we know of God in Jesus, and read the psalms in that light. As St Augustine wrote of Christ:

. . . it is His voice that ought by this time to be perfectly known, and perfectly familiar, to us, in all the Psalms; now chanting joyously, now sorrowing; now rejoicing in hope . . .[3]

But we will not benefit if we try to avoid the truth that these are Jewish prayers and songs, with all that is implied in that fact. Jesus will have prayed these prayers as a Jew. We Christians do well to be reminded of the strong strand of anti-Semitism which has run throughout Christian history, with attendant misrepresentation of the Jewish faith. St Paul spoke of a time when the vision of Jews and Christians could find unity in God. Writing to the Gentile Christians in Rome, he said:

> For if you were cut from your native wild olive and against all nature grafted into the cultivated olive, how much more readily will they, the natural olive-branches, be grafted into their native stock (ROMANS 11:24)

As I have shared in the Passover with Jewish friends, and experienced the bracing, down-to-earth spirituality of Jewish people, I have seen much cause for the Christian to show humility and respect, and realized that we have no cause for boasting. So perhaps it is fitting, as we begin to look at the text, to start with a quotation from a Jewish scholar about the psalms:

> It is not surprising, therefore, that as the Psalter draws to a close the sound of singing grows ever more triumphant and joyous. These men of Israel are praising God that he alone is God and that the gods of the nations are but idols. They are singing because there is One who sits enthroned above the praises of Israel and hears their songs

of gratitude (Ps 22:2). Israel is liberated in her acknowledgement of her relation to a transcendent God, who cannot be fettered by the work of men's hands nor by the sophistries of their thoughts. The true Israel is free in the only freedom available to man . . . She is deeply stirred by the excitement of the holy hour and the ecstasy of the festivals, by the sound of the trumpet and the loud shouting, and by the great processionals, for she comes before God with the memories of the glorious deeds spoken and activated into the present and with the expectations for the future contemporized in holy rituals and glad celebrations.[4]

# PSALM 1
## The Blessed Way

*Blessed is the man who has not walked*
*in the counsel of the ungodly:*
*nor followed the way of sinners*
*nor taken his seat amongst the scornful.*

*But his delight is in the law of the Lord:*
*and on that law will he ponder day and night.*

*He is like a tree planted beside streams of water:*
*that yields its fruit in due season.*

*Its leaves also shall not wither:*
*and look, whatever he does it shall prosper.*

*As for the ungodly, it is not so with them:*
*they are like the chaff which the wind scatters.*

*Therefore the ungodly shall not stand up at the judgement:*
*nor sinners in the congregation of the righteous.*

*For the Lord cares for the way of the righteous:*
*but the way of the ungodly shall perish.*

The psalter begins with the words "Blessed is the man who . . .". What follows is not a legalistic morality but a vision of the way to live with God. In our time, as in many ages, there is often a sense of moral confusion. We live in times of bewildering and unparalleled change. In the face of this turbulence, there are those who want to raise wrecks long since holed and sunk by wars and science and experience, to clean off the silt and sail the boat as if it was equipped to tackle today's world. There are others who look back with scorn on the past and despise the claims made to know the will of God. These people appear to believe that we have to build a totally new ship to guide us through mine-infested seas. I do not believe either approach will do. We have to journey with God through all the choices which confront us – both studying and praying in the history of His dealings with His people, in the vision of the good that is to be found in the Bible, but at the same time living our lives in the present, facing up to the new every day. "Behold I am doing a new thing . . . do you not perceive it?" (ISAIAH 43:19, RSV). The Christian believes that the Spirit of God travels with us throughout all the shock of newness to guide, correct and encourage us. The Way of Blessedness is the life we receive from God and the choices we are able to make in His wisdom and strength.

A young man drives to the chemist in a village. In the back seat of the car, his two-year-old son is strapped safely to the seat. The man stops the car and runs into the shop. He is inside for a few minutes, and the child begins first to cry and then to scream. The man comes out, opening a small packet. He gets into the car, feverishly tearing at the wrapping. Angrily, he tells the child to be quiet. He then takes his fix. He expresses enormous relief, and begins to soothe the small boy in the back. Then he drives home. He lives with his wife and child in a beautiful cottage – money is no object. His wife rushes out to greet them. The baby is crying again, but neither of them notice. His wife needs her fix too.

A stockbroker is reading the details of the previous day's stock market in his *Financial Times*. He looks at the traffic streaming into the city and allows his chauffeur to take the strain. There are big decisions to be made today. He has set his mind on closing the company's branch in Liverpool. There are one or two members of the board who just won't face the economic realities of their situation. They will bring the company down with their resistance to redundancies. He's only got five years to go, and he certainly isn't going to see the empire he has built being threatened by a naïve social audit. There is too much at stake. He has learned to be tough. In a position such as his, a person has to put out of his mind the people who will be hurt by the decision. He will make sure they receive a fair redundancy payment, but like a brigadier in the war he has to wipe off a squadron to save the brigade.

A politician is taking part in a rally against unemployment. There are massed crowds – perhaps as many as eighty thousand people. He is last but one on the list of speakers. He is very much the hero of the crowd, and he is well aware that the noisiest section of the crowd is on his side. He looks forward to speaking. He knows what he will say. He has said it many times before. There is a tremendous sense of excitement in being cheered by so many people – it drowns the thought of what the rest of the world will think of him. At this moment, another politician is speaking and giving the crowd some straight talking. They boo and heckle, and it is impossible for the speaker to continue. Perhaps he should step forward and ask for his colleague to be heard — it would show him to be in favour of open debate and free speech. On the other hand, the speaker is a rival for power, and the chanting mob could now write him off for good. Somewhere inside him the voice of the young idealist is suggesting the right course of action, but the heat of the power and the popularity soon overcomes it.

Life is a million choices. Most of them are small, about everyday things — how to arrange the day, what to wear, what to buy . . . , but many of them are serious, with important consequences. Why do we choose one way rather than another? If one choice seems to be good and the other offends our conscience, how do we find the courage to choose the good? Our choices so often involve other people, especially those closest to us. Where do my happiness and their happiness come into the reckoning, and if there is a conflict, how do we decide what to do? Also, do we know the way — what is right and what is wrong? By what set of values do we make our choices? And what is happiness anyway?

We often look back to, or are told to look back to, times when to a nation or a group the way to live seemed clear, when values were shared by most people, when they were passed from generation to generation. If there have been such times, ours is not one. We live in an age when almost every moral decision is questioned, often producing conflict, very often producing confusion and loss of direction in the individuals making the choices. Into their moral confusion are poured many different streams of moral thought — from different religions, from the media and the press, from the communities in which we live. Some of these streams are strong, sweeping people along with them, whilst others are slower and quieter, and yet others seem to have no coherent direction at all. It is bewildering, and many human beings feel lost in the cross-currents.

Our society is the sum total of us all, and at the national level too, it is not difficult to see the ways in which massive decisions are made without real thought being given to why they are made, where they are leading and what are the values that underpin them. So much is assumed! We operate in the belief that the Christian moral framework still operates in a "Christian country", when in fact most of the people would never actively study Christianity, would not claim to have a working relationship with God and do not feel bound by the values involved in the Christian faith. So we make decisions about nuclear weapons and nuclear power, about education, about genetic experiments, about sexuality, about all the features of life which matter to us, without thinking about or articulating the moral basis for such decisions. The moral criteria used can be such ideas as "market forces", "solidarity", efficiency, nationalism, competition, sectional interests, etc., which in reality are morally neutral. Those who claim the greatest coherence in their moral beliefs often seem to be those who ignore the complexity of things, who, in the strength of their convictions, refuse to receive the insights of others and try to impose their will on everyone else. At the other end of the scale there are those who seem to have little or no moral direction at all; who flounder around and leave others floundering.

Those who do not believe in God have an especially difficult task, because there is no reference point – no ultimate force beyond themselves to act as a critique or encouragement of their moral direction. Life for them is contained within the narrow limits of birth and death, and in one sense they have only themselves and their own groups to answer to. They often have wider sources of values such as "the good of humanity" or the happiness of the greatest number, but in the end they are confined to their own assumptions about what the good of humanity and happiness night be. For them, only the history of man is "given". There are no sources of obligation or perfection beyond the human experience. This, of course, does not mean that such people have no values. Christians are often humbled by the high moral standards and the passionate commitment of the atheist and the agnostic. It is also true that many people who claim to know God often say things that are morally grotesque. It is rather to say that whether we are good, humane, loving people, or selfish, brutal and mercenary, the fact that we believe there is God, or there is not God, is highly relevant to the way we look at life, the way we make our choices and the power we have to live according to our vision. It is not my task to show up the weakness of the atheist's or the agnostic's or even the apathetic's moral stance, but rather to try and say why I believe that it is the life lived with God which begins to make sense of this turbulence. I do not believe that humanists have yet demonstrated how morality makes sense, or is sustainable, without seeing our human drama as played out in the presence of God, with God as our purpose, our direction and our goal.

Not surprisingly, Psalm 1 in the collection of psalms as we have them, begins at this fundamental point and gives a clear answer to the question — how are we to live, what will bring us blessedness? The writer of the psalm was handing on to those who would recite it, or read it, or pray it, the wisdom gained from his own experience, the experience of his worshipping community and the experience of the people of Israel. So the book of songs and poems begins with the words: "Blessed is the man who . . ."

I prefer the translation of the Hebrew word as "blessed" rather than "happy". Blessing is something in our lives which we receive from someone else. Happiness describes a state of mind, of personality, which, in theory at least, could depend only upon a person's own resources. We use the word "happy" far more than the word "blessed". The assumption of the advertisers — and they are expressing what they believe to be the strongest desire of the people to whom they are trying to sell goods — is that happiness is what everyone is looking for. We are shown pictures of happiness as sailing on a beautiful yacht, with a beautiful partner, on a beautiful day. Happiness is to be found in that magic circle. But the questions hover around like storm clouds. Maybe the beautiful partner is someone else's, maybe the boat has been bought with money obtained at the cost of other people's well-being, maybe this long, cool drink is the first of too many. It may happen that the beautiful people construct their perfect life of idyllic happiness, but it only lasts for a short while. Perhaps because their own happiness was their only concern, they turn against each other as soon as their wishes collide. Happiness — even the happiness of the greatest number — can be a self-centred idea, based on contentment, and may exclude a whole range of moral values or virtues. A person may think he is happy when he is failing to do his duty, when he is insensitive to the needs of others, and with almost no concept of what is right or true. I have met and known such people. It's easy to say, "Ah, but they're not really happy", but they appear to be happy in the common understanding of the word.

The word "blessed", on the other hand, suggests a quality of life which combines a rightness of life with that portion of happiness which our lives allow us. It is something to do with the blessing of the One who made us. As a son, it gave me happiness to respond in love to my parents, but it also gave blessing – namely the sense of their love to me and the harmony between us. When Jesus spoke the Beatitudes in the Sermon on the Mount, he was certainly not referring to happiness as we tend to understand it on earth:

> Blessed are the poor
> Blessed are the hungry
> Blessed are those who weep
> Blessed are the peacemakers

These are hardly a group of conventionally happy people – yet they are blessed. They may know some joy, but they will also know grief in the face of the tough arrogance of the world. It may well be that they have to wait for their contentment, their bliss, until they are with God. So with those first words of the psalter, we discover this significant distinction between happiness and blessedness. Blessedness concerns our relationship with God and the way we respond to Him.

The psalm then presents a stark contrast between those

who live according to the will of God and those who do not. As I said in introducing this psalm, the psalmist often talks in black and white terms, as though some people were all good and some were all wicked. This is an idea which does not coincide with reality, because most of us are a mixture of good and bad, and indeed spend a great deal of our lives wrestling to enhance the good in us and to defeat or reduce the bad in us. So I read the psalm as though it is addressed to the alternative people I am or can be. I am always hoping that, almost without my knowing, the better side of my nature may be gaining in the battle, but there are plenty of defeats along the way. It is certainly true of my experience that the defeats bring me into a sort of hell where I hate myself, where I am disorientated, where the world around me seems disfigured.

The psalm begins with the negatives:

> *Blessed is the man who has not walked*
> *in the counsel of the ungodly:*
> *nor followed the way of sinners*
> *nor taken his seat amongst the scornful.*

The company we keep is highly significant. The peer group is a very strong influence. We are in part moulded by the behaviour of the people we associate with. This is especially true of children, but also of adults. There have been religious sects who try to cut themselves off totally from the corruption of people who disagree with them, or might taint their purity. One of the shocking things about Jesus was the company he kept: "Look at him! a glutton and a drinker, a friend of tax-gatherers and sinners!" (MATTHEW 11:19)

Jesus saw the self-righteous as the worst sinners — they

judged others and thought they themselves were the good people. Yet he saw through their masks. Behind their self-righteousness was repressed lust, hate and loneliness. On the outside they were "sheep", but on the inside they were "ravenous wolves". This self-righteousness remains a problem for the Church. Far too often we can be gatherings of the self-righteous, mutually reinforcing each other's judgemental attitudes. Jesus called the Scribes and Pharisees "blind guides". It is clear that Jesus found in the outcasts a more open response to his message of the unconditional love of God. He saw the harlots and tax-gatherers accepting the Gospel before the righteous. I have to say that I have often found more openness, generosity and true godliness amongst those who would not rate themselves highly than in those who are convinced that they are right and know what God thinks.

The psalmist warns against following the advice given by those who damage and hurt others, and aligning ourselves with the scornful. Religious people have often been subjected to scorn. It is the way people deal with their own guilt when they see someone doing what they know they ought to do, or being what they know they could be. Jesus was fierce about scorn — it is essentially the denial of the value and the potential of another person, who is a child of God, bearing the likeness of God.

You have learned that our forefathers were told, "Do not commit murder; anyone who commits murder must be brought to judgement." But what I tell you is this: Anyone who nurses anger against his brother must be brought to judgement. If he abuses his brother he must answer for it to the court; if he sneers at him he will have to answer for it in the fires of hell. (MATTHEW 5:21-2)

So we are not to be swept along by those who deny God or deny the value of others. Jesus himself used satire as a weapon against the self-righteous and the powerful, but never against the down-hearted or the poor or the oppressed.

The psalmist then turns to the more positive content of his wisdom:

> *But his delight is in the law of the Lord:*
> *and on that law will he ponder day and night.*
> *He is like a tree planted beside streams of water:*
> *that yields its fruit in due season.*
> *Its leaves also shall not wither:*
> *and look, whatever he does it shall prosper.*

In order to understand these verses, it is essential to understand two backgrond factors – first, the meaning of the Law (Torah), and secondly to appreciate a climate rather different from our own. For us now, the word "law" conjures up a whole series of meanings, from the bewigged judge sitting in court, to the white car with the flashing blue light coming up behind us on the motorway when we have transgressed, or the same car spotted ahead of us when a whole group of cars is speeding down the outside lane. The "law" to others may mean those rules of our society laid down by Parliament, by acts and precedent. Although there are some similarities to these meanings of law within the Torah, those of us who are not Jews have to make a step of understanding to begin to grasp the value and meaning of the Torah itself.

Just as parents who love their children have in their minds the way their children should live and explore life, so God has in mind how we should live. The parents may say, "No, you may not go near the fire," or "Yes, you can jump from there," or "It's wrong of you to take your brother's toy car and throw it in the pond," or "It's right for us all to give a helping hand." The parents are wanting the maximum freedom for the child, so that he or she may grow into a fully responsible and loving person. Sometimes the child will see the rules and restrictions as being like a prison, and at other times may wish for a stronger and clearer set of instructions. But the purpose of the whole is a full life in harmony with what the parent believes to be the best. But, of course, as far as the parent and the child are concerned, it will not just be a matter of regulations, approving this or approving that, but a great deal will depend upon their relationship. The mother and father who are loving will give many signs of love, encouragement and approval, and probably also at times will be angry and may "judge" what the child is doing. But if the relationship is right, then there will be a sort of grace, a loving energy and context in which the child operates.

In using the analogy of parents to describe the understanding of the Torah, we have to be cautious in two particular ways. First, we have the direct words of our parents, whereas the direct words of God are mediated through human scribes or in the invisible workings of our own minds. Secondly, we realize that we can see the fallibility of ourselves and our parents, and therefore their "law" lasts until we have adult minds to make our own decisions. The Torah is eternal, and our infantile contemporary morality needs to be challenged and judged by the mature wisdom of God's revelation, but our understanding of the will of God will still change and develop, as the human race accumulates knowledge and experience.

The Torah was the accumulated revelation of God's will for the man who trusted God and wanted to follow in God's way. Although there were punishments for disobedience, although God judged the behaviour of His people, nevertheless His love was always in waiting, desiring to guide and strengthen His people. The Torah not only showed the way, but stood for the promise of God to walk the way with us, and therefore was a source of beauty, strength, truth and harmony in life, to be profitably studied and relished. We read in Psalm 19: "The law of the Lord is perfect, reviving the soul" (v7). This is an experience that can be ours through studying and reading not only the psalms, but the whole of the Bible – with its history, its wisdom, its poetry, its teaching, its revelation of the wonder of God.

So living by the Torah was a way of life based upon the study of God's word to His people, the life rooted in the relationship with God through prayer, the life inspired and nourished by expressing our love of God in worship and being assured of His love in return. In the debates about right and wrong, the Bible is often used as a sort of highway code to be referred to, as though it provided answers to particular driving problems. But it cannot work like that if God is not in a real sense the co-driver in all the journey. People are depriving themselves of the nourishment and the wisdom of God through the three millenia of its composition by not reading and studying the Bible on a regular basis. Those Christians who neglect the Bible are admitting their loneliness from God, the Father of our Lord Jesus Christ, or not receiving or accepting His Spirit.

So for the Jew, the Torah is not just laws and regulations, nor a strait-jacket for the character, it is a constant source of guidance, encouragement, inspiration and joy.

The law of the Lord is perfect, reviving the soul:
the command of the Lord is true
and makes wise the simple.
The precepts of the Lord are right
   and rejoice the heart:
the commandment of the Lord is pure
and gives light to the eyes.
The fear of the Lord is clean and endures for ever:
the judgements of the Lord are unchanging
and righteous every one.
More to be desired are they than gold
   even much fine gold:
sweeter also than honey
than the honey that drips from the comb.
Moreover by them is your servant taught:
and in keeping them there is great reward.

(PSALM 19:7–11)

A London taxi driver once told me about his Jewish mother who had lived in Bethnal Green. On the Sabbath she would go without a fire in the biting frost rather than break her discipline about not working on the Lord's Day. She would rather ask a Gentile friend to help her than chop the wood herself. He told me how his faith did not mean much to him now, but I saw in him a sort of regret, almost a longing for something to believe in like that. His mother believed that her life was lived out for God, with God, before God. This gave her a special quality. You could tell that she was, like Abraham, the friend of God. To the taxi driver, his mother's strictness about the Sabbath seemed strange and old-fashioned, yet he wondered what there was in his own life to fill the void of that relationship with the God she loved. He also saw his son growing up without the memory of his grandmother, and he wondered if that hallowed and treasured memory was going to die for ever. "The way" was not being passed on, and there was not that living sense of being in the company of God. That "way" was a great treasure to hand on from generation to generation, and it was absurd to think that each generation would work it all out from the beginning for itself. It would almost certainly run through the same experiences and end up with the same age-old questions, but the treasures of faith would have been left behind in the Jewish cemetery in east London.

As the taxi driver drove away, I wondered if for a moment these words would come back into his mind:

> When your son asks you in time to come, "What is the meaning of the precepts, statutes and laws which the Lord our God gave you?" you shall say to him, "We were Pharaoh's slaves in Egypt, and the Lord brought us out of Egypt with his strong hand ... The Lord commanded us to observe all these statutes and to fear the Lord our God; it will be for our own good at all times, and he will continue to preserve our lives." (DEUTERONOMY 6:20–21, 24)

This text brings together the relationship of the people of Israel with God, the history of the wonderful things He had done for them and the way they should live in response. This is a beautiful and inspiring meaning and context for a life, giving a sense of rootedness and direction. The taxi driver is like many of us, and perhaps our whole generation, who feel a great sense of moral and religious discontinuity with our past, almost as though every age is totally new, as though we were cast off on an island, separated from our past and isolated from God. It is a matter of infinite concern that we have achieved so little in passing on the faith, the sense of history and purpose from genration to generation. Perhaps we had reached a sort of bankruptcy in the terrible wickedness of two world wars and the ensuing materialism. If that is the case, then Psalm 1 becomes even more important, because we all must search for blessedness. We need to base our lives on meditation . . . In that love of God we shall find our way. We need a renewed vision of our daily walk with God and to take seriously the demands and inroads that "walk" makes upon our autonomy and selfishness, in the knowledge that it leads to the liberty and fullness of the children of God:

> *But his delight is in the law of the Lord:*
> *and on that law will he ponder day and night.*

This leads me to verses 3 and 4. The psalmist sees the person who ponders day and night on the Torah as like a tree, planted beside streams of water. In the Palestinian setting, water provides one of the greatest parables of the life which comes from God; whereas we perhaps have a surfeit of water – maybe the sunshine is a stronger image of what we need! After the third week of snow and ice and fog in February, we long for the sunshine which warms and blesses us and makes us feel at peace with our surroundings. In the arid desert the reverse was the sign of the goodness of God.

This was brought home to me vividly when I visited Namibia, where I became seriously dehydrated, and ill as a result. It all happened so quickly, demonstrating again how much our system depends on water. I do not find it difficult to see this as a parable of my dependence on God. Our bodies do not go into shock if we are dehydrated of God, yet the long-term effects on our life and our well-being are as great. During the visit, we stayed on the Angolan border, where we were billeted at the home of Archdeacon Philip Shilongo, who had borne witness to Christ under constant gunfire and bombardment, who had been imprisoned and interrogated, yet remained a tree of righteousness. I asked him, as we were leaving, how it happened that we had running water whilst the drought was so terrible – the cattle were skeletal, the rivers completely dried up and the only source of water was the deep, deep well. He said, with a twinkle in his eye, that they had been saving their water for weeks, so that we could have the tank full, because we were used to it. I remembered how marvellous it had been to have a shower, and felt a pang of remorse for letting the water run away; but most of all I experienced a sense of abiding gratitude.

The psalmist's picture of the concealed water springs watering the deep roots of the tree is important to grasp, because it has within it a source of hope.

I was talking recently to someone who was depressed and disheartened. I tried to listen and let his gloom out of his system, and even give the best advice I could. Somehow the source of his depression lay hidden. He had been given tranquillizers, counselling, the lot, but the source of the depression lay somewhere deep within himself. It is often like that with people – it is when we want to say "Snap out of it," or "Pull yourself together," that we know we have reached the point when our advice and our pills cannot penetrate far enough. I recognize this in myself, and see how faith and love and hope often emerge from below the surface of myself, just as my glooms and depressions are often triggered by a particular event or word or action – yet the source remains subterranean. I think this is one of the instincts that lies behind the experimentation in drugs and cults, because people are searching for something which goes deep enough to tackle their heart – the very springs of their personalities. Religion is undoubtedly concerned with this, and our rites hope to express that deep need for inner life. For instance, we die and rise in baptism in trust that God is able, through our trust, to change our soul, through our spiritual rebirth, clearing away our sin.

Prayer is in part a practice which operates at a subterranean level. Reading the psalms, worshipping in church, receiving the sacraments, are all ways of reaching the unknown spring of ourselves. We are "like a tree planted beside a watercourse, which yields its fruit in season and its leaf never withers". This nourishes our own longing for goodness, love and righteousness, and so inspires the way we live. Jesus told a woman who had drawn water for him from the well:

If only you knew what God gives . . . you would have asked him and he would have given you living water . . .

The water that I shall give . . . will be an inner spring always welling up for eternal life. (JOHN 4:10,14)

Daily prayer and reading of the psalms works like that — it irrigates the soul and we hardly know it is happening, we just become aware of the healing of the tree and the fruit.

This image of the tree bearing fruit is often used in the Bible, for obvious reasons. Healthy trees bear good fruit, unhealthy trees show their disease. Trees depend on their roots. Trees depend upon the reservoir of water given by God for their well-being. Trees grow and give shade to others against the punishing sun. Trees are a sign of plenty. The tree whose leaves will not wither is the one tapped in to the stream. So the human being who will live the full, abundant, blessed life is the one who is rooted in God, open to the Spirit of God, and gives praise and fruit to God.

> *As for the ungodly, it is not so with them:*
> *they are like the chaff which the wind scatters.*

With one of those sharp changes of scene, the psalmist gives us in verse 5 a picture of the farmer winnowing his grain. He throws it up into the wind so that the chaff will be separated and blown away. Those who do not grow in God are likened to the chaff — blown this way and that. It is the claim of the writer that those who turn their back on God will lose their way, and they will not come into God's presence, nor His love, and they will lose hold on life. "The way of the ungodly shall perish" (v7). It is cerainly true of my experience that the ungodly ways in myself lead me to inner isolation, self-pity, and feelings and thoughts that undermine my sense of integrity, rejecting the self God wants me to be. Not only do I lose any intimacy with God, but also despair for a time that I shall be able to find Him again.

*Therefore the ungodly shall not stand up at the judgement: nor sinners in the congregation of the righteous.*

Verse 6 presents a problem for the Christian. The problem recurs throughout the psalter, so we'll face it here. The psalmist appears to be sure that in face of the judgement of God he is righteous. C.S. Lewis, in his *Reflections on the Psalms*, expresses the dilemma in this way:

> The ancient Jews, like ourselves, think of God's judgement in terms of an earthly court of justice. The difference is that the Christian pictures the case to be tried as a criminal case with himself in the dock; the Jew pictures it as a civil case with himself as the plaintiff. The one hopes for acquittal, or rather for pardon; the other hopes for a resounding triumph with heavy damages.[1]

Perhaps it will also help us to understand if we go back to the context and use of the psalm. It has been shown by scholars that many of the psalms were used in the cult of Israel, at events like the anointing of the king, the great festivals, harvests and seed sowing. One such use was to face the congregation with a choice between two ways – the way of God and the way of evil. The people would gather in the congregation and they would be offered the choice of being faithful to the covenant they had made, or turning away from it. Those who were faithful would be blessed – watched over by God – those who turned away were fools and were heading for futility. Rather in the same way as we now make our baptismal vows:

| | |
|---|---|
| Do you turn to Christ? | *I turn to Christ.* |
| Do you repent of your sins? | *I repent of my sins.* |
| Do you renounce evil? | *I renounce evil.*[2] |

No one has ever said "No" when I have asked those questions, though all of us know that young and old alike, who at that moment most earnestly want to live according to their promises, will err again. In the act of worship, in the baptism or confirmation, the person is saying what they most hope and long for in life. This example may help us to understand what in Psalm 1 looks at first sight like self-righeousness and exclusive "holier than thou" claims. They needed to make choices, and indeed needed the sharp word of the consequences of the wrong choice, to help them find the will to choose the right.

At the moment we are seeing a massive campaign to stop young people taking drugs — "Just say 'No'!". The campaign shows horrific pictures of young boys and girls who have said "Yes". Their bodies, their friendships, their well-being, are all totally undermined. The way of heroin leads to destruction, the hoardings are saying. It is the belief of the Jew, and indeed of the Christian, that obedience to and love of God lead to the right life, and that by turning our backs on God we lose our way. There can be no doubt that belief in God makes a difference to our behaviour — or at least to our longing to behave in a loving way. So the worship described in the psalms offers a blessing or a curse, meaning or futility, and invites us to choose blessedness. This may appear to the outsider a more vague and abstract choice than the life or death decision of whether to say "Yes" or "No" to drugs, but to the Jew and the Christian the effects

41

of turning our back on God's will are likely to be just as severe in our relationships, our psychology and our integrity.

The basis of the Christian Gospel is that God cares for sinners. God showed through Jesus that He reached out always for the lost and the fallen, calling them to repentance. We all know that day by day we are part sheep and part goat, part good and part bad. We pray day by day that God will forgive us our sins. It is the centre of St Paul's development of Jesus' teaching that "while we were yet sinners He died for us". All have sinned, and our righteousness is not a state achieved by our own obedience, but by our faith in the love and forgiveness of God. For this reason, the "assembly of the righteous" will contain many sinners. If it was not so, there would not be many left who would qualify. What God looks for is our penitence, not our goodness. Our penitence should lead to goodness, but it can also lead horribly quickly back to the same dreadful old sins. Jesus himself tackled this mistaken self-righteousness when some men brought a woman before him who had been caught committing adultery, threatening to stone her to death. The root of their lack of understanding was their self-righteousness, and he stopped it in its tracks by saying, "That one of you who is faultless shall throw the first stone." (JOHN 8:7) They all sidled off. He told the woman to sin no more. I doubt that, even though she had seen Jesus face to face, she was able to obey him for ever. Those who claim a righteousness of their own are dangerous, because they are blind to their own stains. So when we read verses like this, we should think of ourselves as both godly and ungodly, sheep and goats, and so be warned against the ever-present temptation to believe we are morally superior.

\* \* \* \* \*

*For the Lord cares for the way of the righteous:*
*but the way of the ungodly shall perish.*

This last verse of Psalm 1 is a statement of faith that God watches over our destiny if we live in trust. The Book of Job profoundly questioned the idea that good people inevitably prosper. He knew what we know, that good people often suffer — even seem to attract suffering. The love and goodness of Jesus drew upon Himself the hatred and violence of the people with power around him. But the person who prays and trusts, will nearly always be shown a way of looking at their own situation in hope. It is not success or prosperity which mark out the righteous man, it is their rightness with God. It is a mighty and powerful energy in a life to believe that God watches over our destiny, whatever life throws at us. That basic, simple trust can transform a person's way of looking at their experience. To me, it has been the key to solving my anxiety, a slow cure for resentment, a release of the courage to be and to act, to adventure forth and, in a special way, to be free; whereas to return all the time to absorbing self-concern, self-aggrandizement, self-greed, is to drop into that "slavery" of sin which leads to self-dislike, emptiness and futility.

Every day brings me both freedom and slavery, slipping from one to the other and back as easy as blinking, and this in spite of believing that I have been shown the way to blessedness. There is a strange malfunction in us that, seeing the good and the evil set out before us, seeing blessedness and misery, we still can be fooled again and again into choosing to hurt ourselves and others. I end up praying that God will watch over me whatever fool thing

I do, and hoping that somehow those springs of goodness are watering and refreshing my soul — so that, by a subterranean miracle, I will choose the good.

# PSALM 23
## The Lord is My Shepherd

*The Lord is my shepherd:*
*therefore can I lack nothing.*

*He will make me lie down in green pastures:*
*and lead me beside still waters.*

*He will refresh my soul:*
*and guide me in right pathways for his name's sake.*

*Though I walk through the valley of the shadow*
*of death,*
*I will fear no evil:*
*for you are with me,*
*your rod and your staff comfort me.*

*You spread a table before me*
*in the face of those who trouble me:*
*you have anointed my head with oil and my cup*
*will be full.*

*Surely your goodness and loving-kindness*
*will follow me all the days of my life:*
*and I shall dwell in the house of the Lord for ever.*

This psalm is so important not only because it is a great prayer of the people, but also because it sets out in the simplest terms the character of the trust we are to have in

*The Lord's Song*

God. In a society where many of us are surrounded by layers of comfort and insurance it is difficult to picture the naked trust which is required of those who have nothing, or who live constantly exposed to danger and death. In my experience, faith seems to shine most brightly amongst people stripped of worldly security. This in itself is a challenge to materialism. Yet in a way the psalm is very earthy and reminds us that in life and death our dependence on God must not be hidden or disguised from ourselves by our misleading appearance of self-sufficiency. However much we are committed to progress, to technical development, to the elimination of disease and suffering, they are, in reality, an attempt to reveal and use the wonderful treasures of God's creation. In spite of our incredible advances, we remain children of God bound on this earth by death. By restoring our sense of nakedness before God, we are made to look at what living by faith really means, and to put our trust more truly in Him.

"The Lord is my Shepherd", like many other psalms, is called "A psalm of David". In the first book of Samuel, we are told that when David's elder brothers went off to war, David was in Bethlehem looking after his father's flocks. When he reached the battlefield and saw the giant Philistine, Goliath, he said to King Saul, "Sir, I am my father's shepherd; when a lion or bear comes and carries off a sheep from the flock, I go after it and attack it and rescue the victim from its jaws" (1 SAMUEL 17:34–5). We are also told that David became Saul's armour bearer, and whenever Saul was seized by an evil brooding spirit, "David would take his harp and play on it, so that Saul found relief; he recovered and the evil spirit left him alone" (1

46

Samuel 16:23). So David had a reputation as a musician. We also learn in the second book of Samuel that when Saul and Jonathan had been killed, David made a lament for them: "He ordered that his dirge over them should be taught to the people of Judah" (2 SAMUEL 1:18). It is difficult, however, to say whether psalms attributed to David were written by him — indeed some cannot have been because they refer to events long after his death. At most, we can say that there was a strong tradition that he was a music-maker and composer, and in a way, Psalm 23 would be most appropriate to his life as a shepherd, a fugitive and a king.

The greatest collection and development of the psalms took place in the context of the acts of worship in the Temple. We shall see in Psalm 137 that there were guilds of musicians and singers, and the ascriptions at the beginning of each psalm almost certainly belong to a centuries-long process. Some of the psalms were especially associated with the king, with his enthronement, his health and well-being, his victories and defeats:

> The king shall rejoice in your strength, O Lord:
> he shall exult in your salvation.
> You have given him his heart's desire:
> you have not denied him the request of his lips.
> For you came to meet him with the blessings
>     of success:
> and placed a crown of gold upon his head.
>
> (PSALM 21:1–3)

The king, in a profound way, represented the people, so that they lived out their history, in part, through his life.

47

Scholars argue that this applies both to psalms which are prayers of an individual and also to some which are representative of the whole people:

> Contend, O Lord, with those who contend
>   with me:
> fight against those that fight against me.
> Take up shield and buckler:
> and arise, arise to help me.
> Draw the spear and bar the way against
>   those that pursue me:
> say to me, "I am your deliverer."
>
> (PSALM 35:1–3)

So also there has been discussion about Psalm 23, as to whether it is a psalm of the "Shepherd King" or the prayers of a poet drawn from his own individual experience. In the end, I do not think it matters, Whether the author was David, or a poet, or a priest; if it was used as a private prayer or a prayer of the king, it still has perhaps unparalleled power to engage the heart. We hear in it so many echoes of songs and feasts, of marriages and deaths. It has become our own prayer and the prayer of many generations, whether we are Christian or Jew.

*   *   *   *   *

> *The Lord is my shepherd:*
> *therefore can I lack nothing.*

"The Lord is my Shepherd. That is how I live." These words were once spoken to me by the Bishop of Namibia, James Kauluma, during a confirmation service. He

48

confirmed in the language of the Ovambo people, the Archbishiop of Japan confirmed in Japanese, and I confirmed in English. The place was Odebo in Ovamboland, on the border between Namibia and Angola. Over two thousand people had gathered at St Mary's, in spite of the curfew, the dangers of mines and the "security forces". It was the time of our visit to the churches in Namibia on behalf of the Archbishop of Canterbury. We arrived at the destroyed mission to hear that the South African forces were not only occupying Namibia, but had advanced 250 kilometres into Angola.

I do not know what moved Bishop James to say at that moment in the service, "The Lord is my shepherd. That is how I live." I do know what it meant for him. He had to journey throughout Namibia never knowing for certain whether he would return safely. The roads were mined by both the South West Africa People's Organisation (SWAPO) and the South African forces, and the presence of the military was all-pervasive. He had confronted the army before, they had gone into the churches and terrorized the people, strafing the corrugated-iron roofs, destroying church buildings and property. In 1988 he was shot with rubber bullets for trying to defend schoolchildren from the "South African Defence Force". Within days of his injury he had set off again to the north of Namibia into the war zone. Bishop James was saying that the only way he coped with this life of danger and risk, faced with so many impossibilities, so much sudden death and intimidation, was to live in trust that the Lord was his shepherd – protecting him, guiding him, leading him to safety.

On another occasion, the delegation was late for an

appointment in the far north and was being held up by an army minesweeper clearing the road ahead. Bishop James calmly ordered our cars to overtake, and so the party became voluntary, unprotected minesweepers – unprotected, that is, except by the Lord, their shepherd.

In the surrounding Namibian countryside, the cattle are herded by small boys, and Bishop James' crook was a perfectly natural symbol of the shepherd's care which he, as a representative of Christ, exercised over the people. Rural Namibia has much in common with rural Palestine in Jesus' day, with only the armoured cars, lorries, transistors and mining towns laying a modern industrialized hand on the community. Bishop James visited the kraals and villages, and all the people came and welcomed him who was their shepherd, who in turn lived in belief that the Lord was his shepherd.

But the rural image is difficult to translate in an urban environment. There is so much involved in the rural society which does not apply in the cities and which can even seem absurd in our highly technological world. This is not caused just by our alienation from nature, but also because of the breakdown of so many of the basic assumptions in the community, which were taken for granted in the small rural village and are lost in the massive conurbations such as London.

A poem by Jon Stallworthy describes this difficulty of putting down roots in the concrete city, and the heartache of those who are not only cut off from immediate contact with nature, but also enmeshed in the complexity of the urban environment:

## Psalm 23

### The Barbican Ash

. . . . in this I read
of a tree winched from a wood
to be set in a concrete glade.
Workmen today come packing
its roots with a chemical Spring.
Men are more mobile than trees:
but have, when transplanted to cities,
no mineral extract of manure,
hormone or vitamin to ensure
that their roots survive, carve through the stone
roots, cable roots, strangling my own.[1]

"The Lord is my Shepherd. That is how I live" not only puzzled me because of its difficulty of translation from rural Namibia to urban England, but also because I found it difficult to apply to myself. Although "The Lord is my Shepherd" has been sung at almost every marriage I have been to, and every funeral and many baptisms, and although the crook was put into my hand as a symbol of my new life as a bishop, I wondered whether this rural image of God's care had come home to me. I, unlike Bishop James Kauluma, do not have to face the fear of mined roads, enemy soldiers, beatings and torture. The objects of my fear are less violent, but perhaps more insidious. I fear the anger and poison of people who hate the things I try to say about God, about race, and resources for the inner cities. I fear the seductions of the vested interests, in whatever form, which slowly choke the determination to stand for the truth of Christ as we see it in our community. I fear the seduction of the Church which can so easily collude with the great powers in our society and lose sight of its living-out of the love of Christ, and concentrate all its energy on its own maintenance and survival. I fear our impotence to change both individuals and society to a greater harmony and mutual responsibility. These are all real fears which have to be dealt with in the only way they can be — by love and by prayer. So this puts us right back where we started — do we have the trust, the faith in the Lord God that He will lead us "beside the waters of peace"? Could we say with the psalmist:

> *Though I walk through the valley of the shadow*
> *of death*
> *I will fear no evil:*
> *for you are with me*
> *your rod and your staff comfort me.*

When we go to face our boss, when we encounter racist violence, when we go to take part in a public debate, when we tackle "the powers that be" about some injustice, when we face the compromised Church, when we ourselves are the compromised Church, do we believe and could we say: "The Lord is my Shepherd, that is the way I live"?

When I returned home to east London from Namibia, it was not long before I was brought down to earth by the realities of being a bishop in a society which is largely apathetic about the Church, and a Church which has travelled a long way and taken on board a great deal of clutter. The most striking contrast was in Pentonville prison on Christmas morning. The chapel is always full, for good reasons as well as dubious. I always appear in full dress, and dread the moment of entry, determined to try to be normal in that abnormal situation. As I walked in, the prisoners on remand saw the shepherd's crook, and the response was as natural as it was obvious. They bleated their scorn. In a way, their response was normal and my appearance was abnormal. They were not afraid to express the mockery that others feel. Yet next year I shall continue to wear my mitre and carry my crook, and hope that I shall be able to begin to say why its abnormality can be a sign that the normality we accept so easily is not the whole of life, that our puny bit of history is only a small moment in the life of the earth and that our earth is only a small part of the eternal dimenson of God.

Because people have found the psalms alien to the urban way of life, they have provided contemporary versions like: "The Lord is my probation officer". I think this is a mistake. It is right to dig deeper in the great treasury of prayer which the psalms, as they are, provide. There is a beautiful simplicity about those opening words "The Lord is my shepherd". We have to remember who "the Lord" is for the Jews. He is the great God whose Name is to be feared, who has set the planets in their courses, who is all-powerful, great mystery, a God of wrath and mercy:

> Why, to him nations are but drops from a bucket,
>   no more than moisture on the scales.

(ISAIAH 40:15)

Yet this infinite God who loved and chose Israel was addressed by the psalmist as "my" shepherd. Just as the sheep in the flock were defended and known by name, so the psalmist conveyed the sense of God watching over him as an individual. The belief that infinite God cares for "me" is the spring of faith.

The "shepherd" is a picture of God which often appears in the Old Testament:

> He will tend his flock like a shepherd
>     and gather them together with his arm;
> he will carry the lambs in his bosom
>     and lead the ewes to water. (ISAIAH 40:11)

or Ezekiel 34:11 – 16, where God condemns the shepherds of His people, and in the end promises to be their shepherd Himself:

> As a shepherd goes in search of his sheep when his flock is dispersed all around him, so I will go in search of my sheep and rescue them, no matter where they were scattered in dark and cloudy days . . . I will feed them on good grazing-ground, and their pasture shall be the high mountains of Israel. There they will rest, there in good pasture, and find rich grazing on the mountains of Israel . . . I will search for the lost, recover the straggler, bandage the hurt, strengthen the sick, leave the healthy and strong to play, and give them their proper food.

There are many other examples, and no doubt it was this understanding of the Lord Jahweh as the Shepherd of Israel and of individuals, which we see again in Jesus' teaching: "I am the good shepherd; I know my own sheep and my sheep know me . . . and I lay down my life for the sheep" (JOHN 10:14). This point, that the good shepherd knows and cares for every sheep, is made even clearer by the charming parable of the one sheep who gets lost. The shepherd leaves the flock and goes out searching for the one lost sheep (MATTHEW 18:12 – 14).

"Therefore can I lack nothing" (v1). The fact that the Lord God Himself cares for us is more than we can imagine or hope for. Even though our life may be fraught with difficulty, nevertheless because God Himself is with us, cares for us, guides us, "therefore can we lack nothing". Jesus told a parable about the Kingdom of God. A man found treasure hidden in a field and he gave all he possessed to purchase the field (Matthew 13:44). The knowledge of God, the peace of God, transform our evaluation of the rest of our lives. The heavenly treasure cannot be stolen or decay, the moth cannot get into it nor rust make it old, and it makes so much of what we desire seem irrelevant and superfluous. When the apostles were in prison, they sang praises to God (ACTS 16:25). They had there what they most desired, that is, the presence of God, and who knows, perhaps they were singing "The Lord is my shepherd, therefore can I lack nothing." The love of transcendent God transforms our experience by His light, so that our perspective changes. When a monk or nun takes vows of poverty, chastity and obedience, they are in one sense vows of self-denial, but in another sense they are an investment in that treasure hidden in the field, and made in trust that when we journey with God we lack nothing.

In the psalm, the abundance of God is not ethereal and mystical, but expressed in down-to-earth terms – good pasture, a feast, a cup overflowing with wine. But the overwhelming fact of the Lord being my shepherd makes everything else pale by comparison. The experience of God's love fills our cup and for that moment we want nothing, we lack nothing. "Here might I stay and sing" – like lovers who cannot bear to part, we only want to remain in the presence and assurance of the Lord.

But what of all those times when we do not know the presence of God? I was once talking to a young Christian with muscular dystrophy. Over the ten years I have known him, his condition has grown steadily worse. He said that he could say this psalm and sometimes feel and mean "therefore I lack nothing", but at other times he longed to walk, to be independent, to live the life that others live. Then the psalm becomes an antidote to self-pity. But it makes him angry that he doesn't have enough faith to sing in his prison. It is only too easy for a person in such a position to turn the need for faith into a new law — a stick to beat himself with: "If I was more faithful I would believe I could be cured." But that is to try to force the hand of God, and the psalm only recommends trust that God has our destiny in His purpose. So the faith is a letting go of our own solution and a trust in the shepherding of God. But how do we do it, when our dissatisfaction, our anxiety, drag us back? It is only the gift of Grace which enables us to believe and trust in Him.

\*     \*     \*     \*     \*

*He will make me lie down in green pastures:*
*and lead me beside still waters.*

A simple, beautiful image which brings before each of us pictures from our own lives when we have rested by still waters. For me, it conjures up the mountains in Scotland and their deeper reflection in the loch. Or the Sea of Galilee and a man seated by the lake in the early morning, lighting a fire for his friends. The sounds of the still waters emphasize the silence. With the dawn, my soul opens to the light, and the peace reflects the beauty of God. People live such stressful lives, and seem just to survive in the struggle to keep everything going. Yet I doubt there could be that peace without the testing pilgrimage. The intensity of the silence and the space and the reflection is in part drawn from the release from stress and fatigue. In Tolkien's *Lord of the Rings*, which describes a terrifying journey full of strange beasts and grotesque enemies, the weary travellers come from time to time to the place where there is peace and abundance, the good pastures and the still waters.

\* \* \* \* \*

*He will refesh my soul:*
*and guide me in right pathways for his name's sake.*

This verse, like every verse in this psalm, seems to operate at two levels. There is both the physical, practical level of saving and renewing life, and also the refreshment and recreation of the soul. The Lord is portrayed as guiding and protecting from danger on the journey, but also, by leading the psalmist in the path of righteousness, it is not just his body which is saved and refreshed, but also his soul. This distinction is important in trying to understand our own life. There is the safety we need in facing the risks and dangers in the life we lead, and there is also our need to be right with God. The way God calls us to go can be extremely difficult, but if we are right with God and right within ourselves, it can be tackled. The real source of the gloom may not be the enormity of the task, but our disobedience, because we are refusing to do what we know to be right. We often divert blame for our own sinful attitudes on to some facet of our journey or someone travelling with us, to avoid facing the real source of our unease. Jesus often said to suffering people, "Your sins are fogiven", or "Your faith has healed you". He was not saying that the illness was caused by the sin, but that the sin was fouling up the person's ability to cope or to get well. Sometimes the specific hard task set before us is God's will, but we cannot understand because we are blinded by our own spiritual disorder.

The Lord will guide us in right pathways, says the psalmist, "for his name's sake". The name of God was more than just a name, because, like every name, it expressed the person whose name it was. The people of Israel could speak of a holy place in these terms:

> Then you shall bring everything that I command you to the place which the Lord your God will choose as a dwelling for his Name – your whole-offerings and sacrifices, your tithes and contributions, and all the choice gifts you have. (DEUTERONOMY 12:11)

The psalmist trusted that God's promise was sure, because steadfast love was the character of God, and that was the power in His name.

The name of God was revealed to Moses: "I am; that is who I am" (EXODUS 3:14) – the name of Being and the Source of Being, the name of movement and the source of movement, the name of the Creator and the energy of the creation. In John's gospel we hear Jesus use this name, "I am", over again, and those who heard the way He said it and did not believe, accused Him of blasphemy. "I am the way; I am the truth and I am life" (JOHN 14:6); "I am the real vine" (JOHN 15:1); "I am the resurrection and I am life" (JOHN 11:25). For the Jew, these words carried echoes of the encounter of Moses with God, and therefore entered the Holy of Holies of their faith and became a scandal. John highlights these words, perhaps remembering the way Jesus said them, but also wanting to convey to his readers the purpose of his gospel, that here in the man from Nazareth was the Word of God. This sense of encountering God when encountering Jesus is most beautifully expressed in the post-resurrection meeting with Thomas:

> One of the Twelve, Thomas, that is "the Twin", was not with the rest when Jesus came. So the disciples told him, "We have seen the Lord." He said, "Unless I see the mark of the nails on his hands, unless I put my finger into the place where the nails were, and my hand into his side, I will not believe it."
>
> A week later his disciples were again in the room, and Thomas was with them. Although the doors were locked, Jesus came and stood among them, saying, "Peace be with you!" Then he said to Thomas, "Reach your finger here; see my hands. Reach your hand here and put it into my side. Be unbelieving no longer, but believe." Thomas said, "My Lord and my God!" Jesus said, "Because you have seen me you have found faith. Happy are they who never saw me and yet have found faith." (JOHN 20:24-9)

Thomas, who had naturally been highly sceptical about the disciples' account of the risen Jesus, found in facing the wounded and yet resurrected Christ, the revelation of God. His awestruck words express his recognition, "My Lord and my God!". Jesus' response reaches out to all generations of believers who will recognize in Him the Lord their God. The power of Jesus' name and the power of Jahweh's name were joined for Christians in their first basic creed: "Jesus is Lord". So we say in the creed that He is "God from God". When from within the deep places of ourselves we, not seeing yet seeing, are able to say and long to say "My Lord and my God", it is a statement of His name as well as of our recognition. To speak the name in such a way is to express our love and our recognition of God in Jesus, and to believe in wonder that Christ has made His name to dwell in us. For His name's sake, our Lord and our God, we offer our very selves to Him.

* * * * *

*Though I walk through the valley of the shadow of death*
*I will fear no evil:*

This sentence deserves a book in itself, and as I write, the threat, the fear and the faith of it make me pause. The shadow of death hovers over us in every fear we experience. It is part of our genetic inheritance. It prospers from the moment of our separation from our mother to our fear of falling in old age. For the ancient people, death was an ever-present reality. They knew that in the midst of life we are in death; whereas death for us, for far longer in our lives, is something that happens to other people. Yet however much we try to anaesthetize our fear of death, it still lies in waiting like a spectre.

The shadow of death was for the Jew the threat of falling into Sheol, where the soulless shades dwelt in nothingness. Death threatens us with the possibility of total non-being, the end of our conscious selves. This casts a shadow of anxiety into our hearts, which takes many forms of disabling phobia. So much anxiety is a camouflaged fear of death, and paradoxically the more affluent, cossetted, protected from death we are — the thicker the camouflage — the more the fear emerges in disguise. So many of our fears derive from our parents' fear for us. Their anxiety about us confirms our own fear of the dangers in the world around us, and they see so many more than we do. It is this fear which, having been at first necessary to our survival, can become an all-pervasive threat and imprison a person for life, stultifying self-expression, undermining confidence and giving a permanent sense of anxiety and inadequacy. Thankfully, most people manage to put their fear into proper perspective.

"The valley" also conjures up a place of darkness. Not the gentle valley which the sun blesses, sheltered from the cold wind, but the valley of beasts and the night. The fears and fantasies of the night hours are known to all of us. I remember my first night in Africa and the way shapes and noises magnified into prowlers. But it is a tragedy that in our society so many people live in the valley of the shadow of death, not from fear of wild beasts or pits or falling rocks, but from fear of more modern forms of violence. The spy-hole in the front door through which we look out fearfully at our callers in the city is a sign of the urban valley of the shadow of death.

But life itself produces a full agenda of fear — from schoolday fears of being bullied, to fears of losing love, to fears of miscarriage, of redundancy, of sudden illness, of accident and explosion. We learn about so many disasters and deaths in every part of the world, and over all is the nuclear shadow of total desruction. Whether our fear has a real cause or is just a beast of our imagination, it casts a shadow.

The psalmist makes another important link – that is the relationship between fear and evil. Evil breeds fear, and fear can breed evil. St Paul says that it is evil that gives death its sting. Our sinfulness, therefore, also leads us in to the valley of the shadow. This is not a truth we need to receive second hand. The shadow is caused by something blocking out the light. Something or someone comes between us and the light, and we ourselves are often the greatest obstacle. There is the enemy within and the enemy outside us.

The fear of the enemy within is only too familiar to most people of faith. We are only too aware of the power over us of the things which tempt us. It is quite easy to repent of other people's sins – it is our particular selection that are the trouble. We recognize the familiar subtle arguments of the stirrer and the tempter. But we speak in our worship of being freed from "the slavery of sin". It is the promise of the Lord. Romans 8:15 is typical of the Christian revelation:

> The Spirit you have received is not a spirit of slavery leading you back into a life of fear, but a Spirit that makes us sons, enabling us to cry "Abba! Father!"

It claims that the good relationship frees us from the fear of evil. The "spirit of sonship", the being in filial love of God, frees us from the threat of the power of evil over us. This is true, too, of our human relationships – nothing counters fear more strongly than good, strong, mutual trust and affection. Both love of God and love of our brothers and sisters drive out fear. As I was first writing this chapter, Anglican bishops were taking part in the Lambeth Conference of 1988. The more we prayed together, the more we listened and shared with each other, the more we sensed the fear slipping away defeated for a while. But we all had to return to our own arena and face the evils from without and within. There were bishops who faced detention and imprisonment, bishops who faced persecution, bishops who lived in fear for their lives. But the good relationships with God and each other, and the faith given in such communion, is the strength of God. It is love which is the power of God in Christ, and it is that power which helps us fear no evil.

The psalmist, too, was enabled by the love and mercy of God to put his faith in his Lord. There is this assurance that for the man of faith, God will "be there".

> When you pass through deep waters, I am with you,
>     when you pass through rivers,
>     they will not sweep you away;
>     walk through fire and you will not be scorched,
>     through flames and they will not burn you.
>
> (ISAIAH 43:2)

For the Christian, this is the gift of the Spirit — the making present of the love of God. He will defend us although we go through the valley of the shadow of death: "I will not leave you bereft; I am coming back to you' (John 14:18). Fear is a root of evil, and by it our hearts and minds are threatened, but thanks be to God, His love casts out that fear. This is not to say that we know no fear, but that fear can be defeated because our defender is alongside us — with us — in us.

*. . . for you are with me*
*your rod and your staff comfort me.*

This is our hope. We are travelling with God. When the people of Israel knew that the Ark, the throne of God, was with them, they went into battle with their fears conquered, and it is that assurance of the presence of God which has helped the martyr look up, the tortured hold to his truth, the timid grow strong. Luther has a wonderful description of our pilgrimage:

> If we believe the waters below us depart and . . . harm us not but flee from us . . . and those above us stand up high as though they would overwhelm us: these are the horrors and apparitions of the other world, which at the hour of death terrify us. If, however, we pay no heed to them and pass on with a firm faith, we shall enter into eternal life dry shod and unharmed.[2]

The offer is made to us to be temples of the Holy Spirit if we open the doors of our soul to Christ. As we face whatever are the challenges of our own particular context, we may quietly draw on that inwardness. The promise is clear and may be trusted, expressed by one who knew from experience:

> . . . and yet, in spite of all, overwhelming victory is ours through him who loved us. For I am convinced that there is nothing in death or life, in the realms of spirits or superhuman powers, in the world as it is or the world as it shall be, in the forces of the universe, in heights or depths – nothing in all creation that can separate us from the love of God in Christ Jesus our Lord. (ROMANS 8:37–9)

One of the unexpected signs of this valiant spirit — the Spirit of God inside a personality — is the humour and fun which bubble up like an eternal spring. Just as the child laughs and chuckles in the security of its mother's love, so those who know Christ's presence experience the loving laughter of God. Working as I am privileged to do with rabbis and people of other faiths, I realize that this precious sign of "God with us" is not confined within one faith.

"Your rod and your staff comfort me." It is interesting to me how children seem to accept my funny uniform. I always take my crook into primary schools, and the children know what it is although many of them will never have seen a shepherd, and some have never seen a sheep. It is easy to explain how Jesus called himself the Good Shepherd — and that the good shepherd looked after his sheep, and whatever the personal dangers or temptations, the good shepherd never left his sheep. Then I explain how the hook at the end of the crook was used to put round the lambs' necks to bring them back from danger. In our schools there are always children who are starved of parental affection, and this image seems to touch some deep need in them.

* * * * *

*You spread a table before me*
*in the face of those who trouble me:*
*you have anointed my head with oil and my cup*
    *will be full.*

There is something marvellously earthy about this image of the feast to which the psalmist feels invited by God. For the Jews, the meal is a special time of communion with friends and family and with God. Like so many Jewish pictures of well-being, it is a scene of ordinary life made beautiful by the presence of God. Jesus translated the Passover meal into the feast where He is the host and gives Himself to those who sit at table. In our worship we use a phrase which I always feel is one of the joyful words of our Eucharist: "Happy are those who are called to His supper." As far as we can see, the feasts were important to Jesus, and it is not fanciful to think that he saw such celebration as prefiguring the heavenly banquet. He contrasts His own ministry with that of John the Baptist:

> For John came, neither eating nor drinking, and they say, "He is possessed." The Son of Man came eating and drinking, and they say, "Look at him! a glutton and a drinker, a friend of tax-gatherers and sinners!" And yet God's wisdom is proved right by its results. (MATTHEW 11:18–19)

There is something enriching and affirming of life, that John's Gospel should describe Jesus' first miracle in the context of a wedding feast.

When I think of the holy, happy meals I have shared, I am more than willing to believe that God loves a good feast. To break bread together, to share fellowship, to celebrate special times in our lives, can be a way into that love which God has towards His children, a foretaste of heaven. For Christ, the feast was offered to everyone:

> Then Jesus spoke to them again in parables: "The kingdom of Heaven is like this. There was a king who

prepared a feast for his son's wedding . . . Then he said to his servants, 'The wedding-feast is ready; but the guests I invited did not deserve the honour. Go out to the main thoroughfares, and invite everyone you can find to the wedding.' " (MATTHEW 22:1–2, 8–9)

He approached His death with the assurance that He would join His disciples in the feasting company of Heaven:

I tell you, never again shall I drink from the fruit of the vine until that day when I drink it new with you in the kingdom of my Father. (MATTHEW 26:29)

The shadow, of course, is the hunger and starvation of hundreds of millions of men, women and children in our world, and so there is a provisonality about the heavenly dimension of our meals. There is the question about our affluence and their poverty which should remind us that we may not rest content until all share the banquet. So by this earthly means the psalmist knew his God was with him as host at the table spread before him.

"In the face of those who trouble me". To gloat is not good, but to rejoice in the victory over evil is what the angels and archangels have done through all ages. There are not many human beings who do not relish vindication. When people mock us, or oppress us, or misrepresent us, or appear to have proved us wrong, it is a natural human reaction to "show them" and to glory in victory. The people of faith should know better, because we have been proved wrong before God and have had to rely on His mercy. It is right to trust that God will see us through unpopularity and persecution, but vindication and victory are only won at the expense of other children of God. To be magnanimous in victory is a precious sign of the Kingdom, and one sadly lacking in our world, where so often the vindication is followed by humiliation of the enemy. This image in the psalm stems from a characteristic we have seen before, in which the severity of the struggle for survival leads to both cruelty and something like gloating over opponents. But how understandable it is, as anyone who has fought and won a libel case knows!

"You have anointed my head with oil and my cup will be full." Again here we have the splendour of the presence and love of God in our lives, expressed in earthly symbols. When new Christians come to their bishop for confirmation, and they are anointed with oil, the cross glistens on their foreheads. It is a sign of godly well-being and reminds me of these lovely lines in the Bible:

> The spirit of the Lord God is upon me
> because the Lord has anointed me;
> he has sent me to bring good news to the humble,
>     to bind up the broken-hearted,
> to proclaim liberty to captives
>     and release to those in prison;
> to proclaim a year of the Lord's favour
>     and a day of vengeance of our God;
>     to comfort all who mourn,
> to give them garlands instead of ashes,
>     oil of gladness instead of mourners' tears,
>     a garment of splendour for the heavy heart.

(ISAIAH 61:1–3)

This passage was quoted by Jesus to describe his own

ministry as the anointed one (Luke 4:16 – 19). This anointing by God can be shared – its beauty and plenty poured out for others

> to comfort all who mourn,
> to give them garlands instead of ashes,
> oil of gladness instead of mourners' tears,
> a garment of splendour for the heavy heart.

Or again, the anointing with oil symbolizes the love which issues from the experience of human unity:

> Behold how good and how lovely it is:
> when brothers live together in unity.
> It is fragrant as oil upon the head
> that runs down over the beard:
> fragrant as oil upon the beard of Aaron
> that ran down over the collar of his robe.
>
> (PSALM 133:1–2)

And, perhaps for the Christian above all, in the anointing of Jesus:

> Then Mary brought a pound of very costly perfume, pure oil of nard, and anointed the feet of Jesus and wiped them with her hair, till the house was filled with the fragrance.
>
> (JOHN 12:3)

There is a deeper sacramental meaning in this beautiful act of generosity and it provides a vivid physical sign of the healing balm and wonder of the Spirit of God.

". . . and my cup will be full." The simple words open up in such a lovely way a picture of the goodness and loving-kindness of God which, says the psalmist, "will follow me

all the days of my life". We know that no human life is
totally free of sorrow or grief. But the sense of the love of
God gives such a strong taste of eternal reality that, even
though in our transience and moods and times of faith-
lessness we shall lose that sense of His goodness and
kindness, we feel we can say we know that God will love
us to the end. I remember how disappointed I was the first
time I felt like Cain, shut out of God's favour. But even
Cain as an outcast would have found Christ searching for
him to be reconciled to Abel. Part of what faith discovers
is the underlying assurance that God will not abandon us.
Just as the psalmist said, "therefore I lack nothing", now
he says, "Surely your goodness and loving-kindness will
follow me all the days of my life." The result of being able
to say truthfully to God, "You are with me", is to have that
unquenchable flame alight which the darkness cannot
comprehend nor extinguish.

*       *       *       *       *

*And I shall dwell in the house of the Lord for ever.*

It may be that this is the pious hope of the song writer,
who has found in the Temple the beauty of worship and
the presence of the Lord. He therefore can imagine no
greater joy in life than being in the company of God. As
we wrestle in faith with the impermanence of our lives, the
transience of our feelings, we do not want to let go of the
sense of God within us. We know that we have to return
to the world and face its and our disorder. So, like Peter,
we recognize how good it is to be with God. "And while
(Jesus) was praying the appearance of his face changed and

his clothes became dazzling white." Peter wanted to hold the moment. " 'Master, how good it is that we are here! Shall we make three shelters, one for you, one for Moses, and one for Elijah?', but he spoke without knowing what he was saying." (LUKE 9:29,33)

But their vision passed and they walked together down the hill into the stream of demanding humanity. Even the Good Shepherd, travelling with God, knew what it was like to feel forsaken. So whilst our lives may be scarred by the deepest doubts and sorrows amongst the liberation and joy of faith, we can look forward to the time when we will live in the presence of God for ever, and the shadow of death will be no more.

# PSALM 42/43
## A Prayer to the
## God of My Life

## PSALM 42

As a deer longs for the running brooks:
so longs my soul for you O God.

My soul is thirsty for God, for the living God:
when shall I come and see his face?

My tears have been my food day and night:
while they ask me all day long, "Where now is your God?"

As I pour out my soul by myself I remember this:
how I went into the house of the Mighty One
into the temple of God,

to the shouts and songs of thanksgiving:
a multitude keeping high festival.

> Why are you so full of heaviness my soul:
> and why so unquiet within me?

> O put your trust in God:
> for I will praise him yet
> who is my deliverer and my God.

My soul is heavy within me:
therefore will I remember you from the land of Jordan
from Mizar among the hills of Hermon.

*Deep calls to deep in the roar of your waters:*
*all your waves and breakers have gone over me.*

*Surely the Lord will grant his loving mercy in the day-time*
*and in the night his song will be with me*
*a prayer to the God of my life.*

*I will say to God my rock, "Why have you forgotten me:*
*why must I go like a mourner because the enemy oppresses me?"*

*Like a sword through by bones my enemies have mocked me:*
*while they ask me all day long, "Where now is your God?"*

> *Why are you so full of heaviness my soul:*
> *and why so unquiet within me?*

> *O put your trust in God:*
> *for I will praise him yet*
> *who is my deliverer and my God.*

I have chosen this psalm and the one that follows it because they express most closely the cycle of praying as I have experienced it. "Prayers to the God of my life" have ranged from the despairing cry to shouts of elation, from soaring hope and joy to the depths of grief and self pity. In between these two extremes there has been the daily normality of quieter conversations. Prayer is an activity of the whole person – warts and all. These psalms tune me in to God and the struggle He has with me and I have with Him. My cry "For God's sake do something!", is so often the prelude to a sense of acceptance and a release from anxiety. I have often said to God, "Couldn't you make it all a bit easier?" But that is one prayer that never seems to have been answered in the affirmative!

*As a deer longs for the running brooks:*
*so longs my soul for you O God.*

I did once see a deer in a drought, straining to find water
at a dried up water-hole, but it is not that image which first
comes to my mind when I read this verse. I remember rather,
standing on a hillside with a group of farmers, motor cyclists
and tourists looking down at a rushing stream. We were
talking in whispers and someone said, "There he is." A great
stag came down into the valley. He had already run ten
miles, and the sound of the hounds was not far behind. Just
above us he went into the stream, and we could sense his
relief as the water cooled and revived him. He trotted
downstream, past where we were standing, his great antlers
on his fine head – soon to be mounted and staring with
lifeless eyes at people drinking in the pub. It must have been
some such experience that made Tate and Brady write the
first lines of their hymn based on this psalm:

> As pants the hart for cooling streams
>    When heated in the chase,
> So longs my soul, O God, for thee,
>    And thy refreshing grace.

The psalmist spoke of a hind, not a stag, and the use of
the feminine here adds a touching note of tenderness,
because there are no antlers for self-defence. The creature
looks in despair for the water which will slake her thirst
and cool and revive her tired body. Then she scents the
running brook, the stream which has not dried up, the living
waters.

It is not surprising therefore that the psalmist can use

this picture: "As a deer longs for the running brooks, so longs my soul for you, O God." This is not the cry of a disembodied spirit, it is a flesh-and-blood person yearning for God. There is something very physical about prayer. Not only do we recognize this because of the impact of our surroundings on us as we pray, but also, inside our bodies, prayer engages the whole person. The vaulted ceilings of an ancient church steeped in prayer communicate with the senses, just as the first grey light at dawn awakens our spiritual perception, and the hurricane whipping the seas stirs the dread in us, or as the soft delicate texture on an old person's arthritic hand moves us to pray, and thus to God. So prayer opens us up as we engage our eyes and ears and touch, and live out our physical human life in God's world. But prayer is also physical in that it is an activity of our whole personality – body, mind and spirit. Our breathing, our desiring, our striving, our relaxing, our loathing, our lusting, our loving, our laughing and crying are the conversation or conflict of our self, our soul, with God. I do not shut my eyes, kneel down and put my hands together when I pray to shut out the physical, but to tune the physical in to God. I shut my eyes because I am engaged in inwardness with God. I kneel because I am expressing my dependence and smallness before God, and put my hands together or hold the palms upwards to remind me that I am looking towards the King of Heaven and waiting to receive Him to myself. A soul is not a disembodied spirit, it is the whole self in relationship with God. Therefore nothing may be excluded – no section of our experience is free of God, and we should expect our prayer and our soul to have a profound effect upon our physical lives. I have no remaining doubt that prayer can cure, can lift depression, can even rebuild damaged cells. It is this same interplay between the soul and the body which makes me hold such an incarnational, embodied, spirituality. It must be partly for this reason that the Lord Jesus gave Himself to us — not just in the promise of the Spirit, but in those elements of our physical lives — our physical survival, our food and our drink.

The hunted deer is harassed by hounds and humans and longs to find rest and safety. So, in a sense, the psalmist too feels surrounded by enemies, by the aggressive world, and longs to find God in whom he may rest. We too battle in this arena of struggle and temptation, and have to find our strength in the glimpses of God we are given along the way as a foretaste of heaven. "I am athirst in my pilgrimage, in my running; I shall be filled on my arrival."[1] Our restlessness and heaviness of soul derive from the contrast between our small transient being and the Being of God in His eternal dimension. St Augustine searched for God in His creation and in his own self, but God was beyond his searching: "Having therefore sought to find my God in visible and corporeal things, and found Him not, having sought to find His substance in myself . . . and found Him not, I perceive my God to be something higher than my soul. Therefore that I might attain unto Him."[2]

By comparison with our mind which is capable of progress and decay, knowledge and ignorance, remembering and forgetting, God is unchanging and infinite. So, says St Augustine, we are always on this earth in a state of longing for the heavenly place of God, from which we have heard music and sensed the light, and towards which we journey.

"His dwelling place is above my soul; from thence He beholds me; from thence He created me; from thence He directs me and provides for me; from thence He appeals to me, and calls me, and directs me; leads me in the way and to the end of my way."[3] The writer of the letter to the Hebrews puts it like this: "For here we have no permanent home, but we are seekers after the city which is to come." (HEBREWS 13:14)

\*   \*   \*   \*   \*

*My soul is thirsty for God, thirsty for the living God:*
*when shall I come and see his face?*

"My soul is thirsty for God." "So longs my soul for you, O God". These passionate, emotional words seem rather far removed from the precise neatly suited, pin-striped buttoned-up religion which we often see, at least externally, portrayed in church. It is not surprising that the young people find our worship dessicated – so many words without passion! "Longing" and "thirst" are the words of the lover, the prophet, the lonely. They are words of need, of yearning. "I thirst," said Christ from the cross (JOHN 19:28), yet He would not take the drink offered to Him though His whole being cried out for it. "My heart is ready to break with grief," He cried in the Garden of Gethsemane (MARK 14:34). He looked at Jerusalem and said, "How I have longed to gather you under my wings" (MATTHEW 23:37). He continually allowed prayer to break into His hectic life. At the tomb of His dead friend, in the face of the hypocrisy of His accuser, in His grief at the people's blindness, in the face of the leper, He was continually expressing His need of God and praying with longing — thirsting for the reality of God to spring from the deep eternal well.

We are made for relationships with God and with each other. We search for rest and fulfilment in both. The Lord God said, "It is not good for man to be alone" (GENESIS 2:18), and Adam was given Eve to be with him. But both Adam and Eve were intended not only to be in close, loving, longing relationship with each other, but also with God. We are not made to be alone, and so in our inmost selves we yearn for a partner to love, and we are not made to be alone from God, but in our inmost selves we yearn for Him. To me, it is a source of wonder that the Bible often compares prayer, obedience, faithfulness with the love of human beings for each other — husband and wife, father and son, and friends.

So I understand my relationship with God in a very physical, whole-self way. The word "spiritual" refers to that dimension, capacity, relationship which our whole self can have with God. Our prayer is the expression of that relationship as we look for a cure for our soul, and God responds through the knowledge, the thought and the feelings which we can share with Him. He is the living God, the running spring which never dries up, the eternal, deep and pure well, the total source of love. I believe that in Him we can find eternal friendship, and a promise of that wholeness and transfiguration which is to be our life with the risen Christ. But in this journey we struggle and recognize the cry of the psalmist: "When shall I come and see his face?"

Have you had the experience of longing to see the face of someone you loved and depended upon, who has died? You go and look at his/her photograph, but it is not enough.

I remember the panic of not being able to picture my mother or my father, and the tremendous comfort of seeing them in a dream. In a magazine the question was asked, "What most attracts you to a person?" My answer would always be "their face." The face, and the eyes in particular, are the way in to knowing a person. Jesus said that the eye was the lamp of the body – not only the way we look out to the world, but also the way the world looks in on us. The face shows the fun and the suffering, the insecurity, the confidence, the hardness, the compassion. It is therefore to be expected that people seeking God would say they seek "to see his face". St Paul described the longing in this beautiful way: "Now we see only puzzling reflections in a mirror, but then we shall see face to face." When we love someone, it is enough to be with them, it is enough to gaze into their eyes, to receive their love for us, to be bathed in their love for us, to come to that intimate togetherness which does not need words, where we know and are known and are no longer alone: "My knowledge now is partial; then it will be whole, like God's knowledge of me" (1 CORINTHIANS 13:12).

But of course there is another side to being in the presence, before the face, of the one we love. It can make us want to hide. Those eyes seek ours and we are ashamed. We all remember the desolate feeling of going to our parents with some dread confession. It is the human instinct to lower the eyes and not dare to look the person in the face. How much more would this be true with God. The Old Testament recognizes this awfulness of being looked at by God. Adam and Eve cannot bear to face Him, so they hide in the garden He gave them. Jacob spends a lonely, troubled night wrestling with a stranger and he named the place Peniel "because," he said, "I have seen God face to face and my life is spared" (GENESIS 32:24–30). But above all, the awfulness of looking upon the face of God is described in Exodus 33:18–23. When God had revealed His name to Moses He made all His goodness to pass before him. God said "My face you cannot see, for no mortal man may see me and live . . . you shall see by back, but my face shall not be seen." Even so, Moses' face shone because he had been speaking with the Lord, and when Aaron and the people of Israel saw how the skin of Moses' face shone, they were afraid to approach him. Even the reflected light was too much to look at.

For Christians, God in one sense has a face – the face of Christ. Karl Barth described him as "the humanity of God". This face of Jesus has a significant part to play in our spirituality. Though science may have proved the Turin Shroud to be a pious fake, the fascination which it still holds for many people expresses the forlorn hope to see His face on earth. That face has been portrayed in innumerable ways by every race – a universal man. Those faces have been created in the imagination of artists and sculptors, in their prayers and from the reading of the Gospel narratives. So often we see Jesus looking at a person, seeing through their soul. Before that face the leper saw himself as healed, the prostitute saw herself as forgiven, the hypocrite's mask was no use, the virtuous rich young ruler discovered his poverty. Pilate saw no guilt in His eyes, and poor Peter wept when he saw that look when the cock crew. There are so many glimpses of the face of Jesus that we almost feel we know Him, and through His eyes we can look into the "eye" of God.

\*   \*   \*   \*   \*

*My tears have been my food day and night:*
*while they ask me all day long, "Where*
*now is your God?"*

Before our days end we shall all know the experience of
tears as our food day and night. Most of us know what it
is like to feel that ache around the eyes, that sense that grief
will never leave us; when even our crying does not free us,
when the night becomes a place of deepened sorrow, and
our weariness and sense of loss prevent even our sleep. I
have come to believe that our different sources of grief flow
into one reservoir in our soul. So one grief can release others
and something quite trivial – like the loss of a photo or
a gift – can open a floodgate.

The psalmist has a particular grief in mind, the apparent
absence of God. He feels hounded and persecuted, driven
into a corner, but the taunt which hurts most is, "Where
now is your God?". This scorn was hurled at the dying Jesus;
"He saved others, but he cannot save himself. Let him come
down now from the cross, and then we will believe him.
Did he trust in God? Let God rescue him, if he wants him"
(MATTHEW 27:42). So many times a picture of Christ comes
to mind as we read the psalm "Where now is your God?"
The psalmist feels God-forsaken. He had trusted in God,
but still he was experiencing defeat and stress. It is not hard
for the believer – in almost any faith – to identify with
this feeling, and it is only too easy for the priest and the
bishop in a secular society to identify with the pain. I
remember so many times when I have felt a fool, when
situations have seemed hopeless and God-forsaken, when
I felt the power of the question within myself: "Where now

is your God?" I recall the grief-crazed parents of a beautiful twelve-year-old who died of leukaemia. Their only child was lying in bed surrounded by all the gifts they had lavished upon her out of adoration – they looked on her pale face, next to a lifeless cuddly toy. "Where now is your God?" I remember a dear friend who slowly grieved for her husband and one night, without a reason left to live, she lay down in her kitchen and died. I remember a sixteen-year-old-boy who absurdly drove a car round a field, lost control and in a moment of foolishness ended his life. "Where now is your God?" I remember all those people – some apparently so confident that they could live without God, some so convinced that if there was a God He had opted out of their lives. I know others who seem so good without expressing a need of God and others who in their arrogance shut Him out. But it is not just in the lives of others that I hear the taunt "Where now is your God?" I also find I sometimes say it myself. I cannot understand why God does not seem to answer my prayers to change me; why it takes me so long to tackle the inadequacies of my soul; why it is that so often the good and the innocent and the specially beloved of God die, or seem to be loaded with extra burdens. The power of the taunt is in our own doubt. "Where now is your God?" only strikes home when we ourselves feel God-forsaken.

\* \* \* \* \*

*As I pour out my soul by myself I remember this:*
*how I went to the house of the Mighty One*
*into the temple of God,*

*to the shouts and songs of thanksgiving:*
*a multitude keeping high festival.*

The psalmist poured out his soul to God, and as he did so, his mind turned to earlier, happier days when he went to worship God in the Temple and found the sense of the mighty presence of God. Many commentators accept a different translation here and suggest that the psalmist had been in an honoured place in the worship. Weiser renders it "How I went in procession to the house of God in the company of the exalted"[4], and the RSV translation reads "How I went with the throng and led them." It seems more likely that he was describing the wonder and thrill and exaltation of being with a vast crowd of people worshipping God, carried away by the shouts and songs of thanksgiving.

He remembers the high festival, the time when God seemed close, when he felt the strength of his fellow believers. People of faith need such occasions in a secular world, and I know how many times I have been lifted by that spirit which comes from the congregation in full song. Then we can say, "The Lord is here!"

> Lift up your heads O you gates
> and be lifted up you everlasting doors;
> and the King of glory shall come in.
> Who is the King of glory?
> the Lord of hosts he is the King of glory!
>
> (PSALM 24:9–10)

There is prayer alone and there is prayer with the people of God – there is prayer in the secret room and there is prayer in high festival. St Augustine speaks of the music of the Temple as conveying a distant echo of the heavenly:

> The angelic choir makes an eternal "holiday": the presence of God's face, joy that never fails. This is a "holiday" of such a kind, as neither to be opened by any dawn, nor terminated by any evening.[5]

Because we are still groaning here in the frailty of flesh, we lose the sound of heaven and come back to the din of earth:

> . . . even though we have some way or other dispersed the clouds, by walking as longing leads us on, and for a brief while have come within reach of that sound, so that by an effort we may catch something from that house of God, yet through the burden, so to speak, of our infirmity, we sink back to our usual level, and relapse to our ordinary state.[6]

To the psalmist, these memories make him both long for their reassurance, and rage at himself for continuing to be so depressed.

> *Why are you so full of heaviness my soul:*
> *and why so unquiet within me?*
> *O put your trust in God:*
> *for I will praise him yet*
> *who is my deliverer and my God.*

This chorus, which appears also at the end of this psalm, and again in Psalm 43 verses 5 – 6, is the main reason why these two psalms are seen as originally two parts of the same psalm. Although it is a chorus, the words and their meaning go profoundly to the root of faith. I could not count the number of times I have turned to these words, because they speak so accurately to my condition.

The question I ask myself is, "Why is my soul full of heaviness?" What is the root of my problem? Where did it begin, and what triggers it? St Augustine had no soft answer for his and our disquiet — "it is pride that causes this 'disquiet' "[7]. "By the Unchangeable my soul was revived; it is by the changeable it is disquieted."[8] The enemies we have, place us in one sort of pain, but our own soul entertains the enemy within us. "Thou complainest of the enemy. It is true he does harass thee; but it was thou didst give place to him"[9] So the remedy lies within us: "Iniquity is the cause of thy mourning; let 'Righteousness' be the cause of thy rejoicing! Thou wouldst sin; and yet thou wouldst fain not suffer."[10]

There is an element of rebuke in this refrain. How can a person who has tasted God and heard and seen a glimpse of the heavenly dimension still be miserable? When I list all the blessings of my life, when the love of God has so often been clear to me, when I have experienced the happiness and encouragement of worship and prayer, how can I be so unquiet? I am capable of having nine-tenths of my life content, yet spending long hours depressed by the tenth of my life that is not. This seems disloyal to God, and plain selfish. I have met and counselled many people who are like that, and indeed I suspect that most of us recognize the ungrateful state. It is brought home to me most strongly when I spend time with someone for whom nine-tenths of their life is filled with pain, sickness and trouble, and yet through their faith, they constantly return to the one-tenth which is fine. "There are other people so much worse off." "I'm just thankful I can read." "I'm very lucky you know, I have a home help."

But whilst we all tend to get our own troubles out of proportion, we also have to face heaviness of evil, unquiet feelings which relate more comprehensively to our whole lives. The fears of many of the people suffering from depression — either chronic or temporary — have revealed to me, if I did not already know, what it is like to look into the pit. The psalmist gives himself a talking-to and reminds himself of the way he has discovered freedom from this heaviness of heart in the past.

> *O put your trust in God:*
> *for I will praise Him yet*
> *who is my deliverer and my God.*

That is the act of will which can shake off the coiled self-pity. It is not an easy, nor a trite solution, but rather an appeal to the best in a person, where that best meets up with the power that God has to offer. In a way it is a reminder that in the past we have travelled this way before, and as we struggled, faith lifted us out of the quicksand and set up back on firm ground. It is a command issued to the self in strong terms: "O put your trust in God!" The one person to whom you are allowed to say "Pull yourself together" is yourself. The psalmist looks forward to the time when he is freed of the cold, dispiriting presence and will find his sail filled again with the Spirit, will return to worship and adore. Then he can be delivered from the shadow and be restored and reconciled with God.

\* \* \* \* \*

*My soul is heavy within me:*
*therefore I will remember you from the land of Jordan*
*from Mizar among the hills of Hermon.*
*Deep calls to deep in the roar of your waters:*
*all your waves and breakers have gone over me.*

There is some confusion here as to the meaning of these verses and their translation, and commentators much more learned than I differ over what they mean. The most convincing solution sees the psalmist as remembering his deliverer – his God – from the mountains when he was unable to go to the Temple and where he found himself alone and cut off from God. He summons up his faith and courage as he stands by the source of the Jordan, but instead of seeing the river as the river of life, the rushing image of God's eternal power, he sees the waters overwhelming him, drowning him, buffeting him. He can hear the echo of God in the deep, but cannot resist the flood, and he feels he is going to be swept away by the waves and the breakers, engulfed by the rapids. Psalm 40 speaks of the answer of God through prayer to this fear of drowning:

He brought me up from the pit of roaring waters
out of the mire and clay:
and set my feet upon a rock and made firm my
    foothold.                    (PSALM 40:2)

Here, too, the psalmist moves from the sense of being overwhelmed, to a new sense of faith and assurance:

*Surely the Lord will grant his loving mercy in*
*    the day-time:*

*and in the night his song will be with me*
*a prayer to the God of my life.*

Through this spiritual battle, his struggle with his fears and his heaviness of soul, through the overwhelming flood, he comes to a place of greater peace and serenity. Whereas in verse 3 he says "My tears have been my food day and night", now he can see his day and his night filled with the presence of God. To experience the song of God in our self is to know for a time a personal harmony where we are at one with God — not out of tune, not struggling for the notes, but filled with His song. The verse concludes with the phrase "a prayer to the God of my life", and in a way that is what we search for. Behind our confusion and doubt, our struggles and our wrong-doing, we search for the God of our life. Somehow we know that every part of our life is to do with its source, but all the temporal clutter and conflict obscures the light. And then, through grace, through the bewildering noise, we come into song, and a prayer of love and adoring joins us with the Lord. We know for a while that we are in touch with the source of our being, we are at home, in harmony, singing God's song in a prayer to the God of our lives.

But the moment of assurance when the psalmist had said "Surely . . ." is followed by the conflict, as it so often is in our own lives.

*I will say to God my rock, "Why have you forgotten me:*
*why must I go like a mourner because the enemy*
*    oppresses me?*
*Like a sword through my bones my enemies have mocked me:*
*while they asked me all day long, 'Where now is your God?' "*

Though some of this psalm suggests a degree of introspection, it is also plain that much of the psalmist's distress is caused by his enemies, by people who scorn him and oppress him. It often happens that people's criticism and anger against us stir up our anger against ourselves. His enemies accuse him of being faithless, and indeed he suspects he is weak and vacillating, and so in the face of their criticism he claims help from God, his rock. "I will say to God, my rock . . ." suggests a determination to call God to justify him in the face of his opponents. Like Job, he rebukes God for leaving him, abandoning him to mourning and injury. How totally human, how totally understandable! We see no sign of the psalmist's own guilt, which is probably the main cause of his unquiet and heavy soul, but in the end a challenge to God to live up to His promises: "If I have believed you, served you, given my life for you, then vindicate me – stand up for me – rout the enemy." It is not a very moral prayer, but so recognizable, and God recognizes and understands and receives our prayer.

" 'Why have you forgotten me?' So cried our Head also, as if speaking in our name."[11] St Augustine hears again, in these words, the timeless pleading of Christ.

As the psalmist contemplates the pressure and opposition and hatred of his foes, he repeats the refrain, as he struggles to face up to his despair, and tries to conjure up the only thing that can save him – his trust in the God who delivers him.

## PSALM 43

*Give judgement for me, O God*
*take up my cause against an ungodly people:*
*deliver me from deceitful and wicked men.*

*For you are God my refuge; why have you*
*    turned me away:*
*why must I go like a mourner*
*because the enemy oppresses me?*

*O send out your light and your truth and*
*    let them lead me:*
*let them guide me to your holy hill and to*
*    your dwelling.*
*Then I shall go to the altar of God*
*to God my joy and my delight:*
*and to the harp I shall sing your praises*
*O God my God.*

> *Why are you so full of heaviness my soul:*
> *and why so unquiet within me?*
> *O put your trust in God:*
> *for I will praise him yet*
> *who is my deliverer and my God.*

"Give judgement for me, O God." When the things we say or do are misrepresented, twisted and distorted, a sense of injustice boils up inside because "like a sword through my bones my enemies have mocked me" (PSALM 42:12). But most of us in this country live in relative security. Words like these must be all the more powerful in the heart of a prisoner of conscience, or a hostage, or a refugee. The psalmist reminds God that He is his refuge, his sanctuary, and pleads that God will stand by him and give him justice. Living in a relatively free society, this is a prayer that usually makes me think of others — of the children facing the armoured cars in Soweto, of the people suffering from harassment, of people living in refugee camps around the world, of the *refusniks* — compared with them, our "enemies" and "deceitful and wicked men" are lightweight and hardly worthy of such a description, yet it still can feel hurtful and unfair. But the psalmist finally gets it all out of his system, finishes his moaning and asks God in a simple and straightforward way for His light and His truth.

\* \* \* \* \*

> *For you are God my refuge; why have you turned me away:*
> *why must I go like a mourner*
> *because the enemy oppresses me?*
> *O send out your light and your truth and let them lead me:*
> *let them guide me to your holy hill and to your dwelling.*

In the face of all the opposition and the enmity, he knows that the only answer lies in the truth and the light of God. These are the only weapons we have to fight the trauma and oppression in our lives — the only way to discover our integrity. They can restore our sense of value and identity. When facing up to the scornful "Where now is your God?", the hope arrives when in some way we see our situation, and indeed our enemies, transfigured by the light and truth of God. Many an apparently hopeless situation has been changed by people of faith seeing it transformed by the God in it. There is a glory in the Cross for those who have eyes to see — so there is a glory to be found in many crosses in our world, even alongside the apparent remorselessness of the suffering and evil of mankind. St John's Gospel portrays Christ as the Light and Truth of the world. There He promises that, if we believe in Him, He will guide us into the Truth and the Truth will set us free. In this way the oppressed find the great armoury which is necessary to resist the power of evil in this world. "All that came to be was alive with his life, and that life was the light of men. The light shines on in the dark, and the darkness has never mastered it . . . So the Word became flesh; he came to dwell among us . . . full of grace and truth." (JOHN 1:3–5,14)

For the Jew who wrote this psalm, it was the light and truth of his Lord which would lead him back to the place of God – "to your holy hill and to your dwelling". So he saw that God would guide him back to Zion where he would join the multitude in keeping holy festival, and where he would be vindicated by the presence and affirmation of the Lord his God.

\* \* \* \* \*

*Then I shall go to the altar of God*
*to God my joy and my delight:*
*and to the harp I shall sing your praises*
*O God my God.*

And now the writer has come through to triumphant faith. These words are used by priests as a preparation for celebrating the Eucharist. They have seemed strange sometimes at 7 am in a cold church with just one parishioner as congregation, or when my soul is heavy and unquiet, or when I am too tired to feel anything, and yet they act as a reminder of the triumph of the Spirit of God in the spirit of Man. In the face of the disappointments and the mockery, and perhaps even the apparent absence of God, faith wins through, and we sing the praise of God and experience again that wonderful delight and joy, which come to those who find their way to the altar of God with trust in their heart.

For a certain sound from above so strikes in silence, not on the ears, but on the mind, that whosoever hears that melody is filled with loathing of corporeal sounds, and the whole of this human life is to it but a kind of din, interrupting the bearing of a certain strain from above, passing sweet, incomparable, and ineffable.[12]

# PSALM 46
## The City Of God

*God is our refuge and strength:*
*a very present help in trouble.*

*Therefore we will not fear though the earth be moved:*
*and though the mountains are shaken in the midst of*
   *the sea;*

*Though the waters rage and foam:*
*and though the mountains quake at the rising of the sea.*

*There is a river whose streams make glad the city of God:*
*the holy dwelling-place of the Most High.*

*God is in the midst of her*
*therefore she shall not be moved:*
*God will help her and at break of day.*

*The nations make uproar and the kingdoms are shaken:*
*but God has lifted his voice and the earth shall tremble.*

*The Lord of hosts is with us:*
*the God of Jacob is our stronghold.*

*Come then and see what the Lord has done:*
*what destruction he has brought upon the earth.*

*He makes wars to cease in all the world:*
*he breaks the bow and shatters the spear*
*and burns the chariots in the fire.*

## The Lord's Song

*"Be still and know that I am God:*
*I will be exalted among the nations*
*I will be exalted upon the earth."*

*The Lord of hosts is with us:*
*the God of Jacob is our stronghold.*

I remember praying to God in Hyde Park that I would work anywhere He wanted me to – but not London. I have been in London for most of my life since I prayed those words. Whenever I think about the City of God, I think about London. This is not because I believe that London is the City of God; far from it – but because I have encountered the City of God in London on countless occasions and it is faith in that divine City which keeps me going. The Stepney banner shows the River Thames flowing along our southern border under Tower Bridge and down to Wapping and the Isle of Dogs. The river shivers and glistens and, just as the old river brought myriad life from all over the world to east London, so I believe "the river of the water of life" brings the City of God to us now. This wonderful psalm presents us with the hope that in the face of a turbulent world, though the earth be moved and the mountains quake, the one secure unshakeable place is the City of God, where the holiest of holies is to be found, where God makes His dwelling. This is the "Faith in the City" which keeps our eyes fixed upon the future and draws us on to work for the Kingdom of God on earth as in heaven. Jerusalem stands high and lifted up above the flood and chaos; so too the City of God towers above the maelstrom of our earthly city.

\* \* \* \* \*

## Psalm 46

*God is our refuge and strength:*
*a very present help in trouble.*

Jews and Christians have at the heart of their worship the
recital of the wonderful things that God has done in the
past. In the Passover the Jews recall how the God and Father
of us all acted to save His people Israel from slavery in Egypt.
In the Communion service, Christians eat bread and drink
wine in remembrance of Christ's passion and resurrection.
But it is not just a remembering, it is also reminding
ourselves that He is with us today. Just as He gave the victory
to his people in Egypt, and sacrificed Himself in Jerusalem,
so now in remembering Him, in reciting the deeds of the
past, we encounter Him in the present. He is the only place
of safety in a dark trembling world — "God is our refuge
and our strength." He has shown His love for us so often
in the past, we can trust Him. He is as real now, re-creating
the universe, as He was when He called it out of nothing
to be itself. Compared with Him there is no other true
refuge, no other invincible strength. If, when we are faced
with danger or despair, we trust in Him, He will be "a very
present help in trouble".

\* \* \* \* \*

*Therefore we will not fear though the earth be moved:*
*and though the mountains are shaken in the midst of*
*the sea;*
*Though the waters rage and foam:*
*and though the mountains quake at the rising of*
*the sea.*

97

The psalmist was not just talking about his own little domestic problems. He had the whole creation in his mind. Somewhere stored in the human psyche, there is a memory of the turmoil through which the earth was created. "God spreads the canopy of the sky over chaos and suspends earth in the void" (JOB 26:7). The creation had within it the primeval monster which symbolized the massive brute power of unbridled nature emerging from the sea which God alone could control: "But thou, O God, thou King from of old, thou mighty conqueror . . . thou didst crush Leviathan's many heads" (PSALM 74:12–14, *NEB*). God's power was so great that when He set about creating the earth with flood and volcano and chaos, He was able to bring order and set everything in its place. Because He is that God – the God of all creation – "Therefore we will not fear though the earth be moved and though the mountains are shaken in the midst of the sea; though the waters rage and foam, and though the mountains quake at the rising of the sea."

As we shall see in Psalm 104, there is highly relevant and contemporary comfort to be drawn from this faith. We are a generation who realize the vulnerability of the earth within the universe. Every news bulletin highlights interconnected global damage – the loss of the rain forests, the holes in the ozone layer, the "greenhouse effect", the rising waters of the earth, and behind it all, the threat of nuclear war. This psalm speaks to our anxiety about the environment and the future of the world. There are grounds for our fear that the earth will be changed. The faith of the psalmist reminds us that the universe and the earth itself were brought into being by God, and just as He was in everything from the beginning, He remains the generative power of all things. This does not let us off the hook of our stewardship of the earth, but it provides us with the perspective which calls us to action as those entrusted with the earth by God. So the Lord who drew creation out of chaos is our refuge and strength – a very present help in trouble, "though the earth be moved and though the mountains are shaken in the midst of the seas."

\* \* \* \* \*

*There is a river whose streams make glad the city of God:*
*the holy dwelling-place of the Most High.*
*God is in the midst of her*
*therefore she shall not be moved:*
*God will help her and at break of day.*

Rising triumphant out of chaos, turbulence and earthquakes, is the City of God, Jerusalem standing high on its hill so that the pilgrims look up at its walls, its Temple and its teeming life. It was and remains the sacred place where God the Most High has made His dwelling. Even though Jerusalem was often in enemy hands, partly in ruins, with the Temple destroyed, their faith affirmed that God would restore it, if the people were obedient. The restoration of Jerusalem was symbolic for Jews of the steadfast love of their God who kept covenant. Zion became the focus of Jewish hopes, and features repeatedly in the psalms. This was not only because the psalms themselves were collected and developed within the worship of the Temple, but because the Jews believed that Zion was God's chosen city. Here are some examples:

The Lord is great and worthy of our praise
    in the city of our God, upon his holy hill.
Fair and lofty, the joy of the whole earth
    is Zion's hill, like the farthest reaches of
      the north,
    the hill of the great King's city.
In her palaces God is known for a tower of
    strength.              (PSALM 48:1–3, NEB)

God shines out from Zion, perfect in beauty.
                      (PSALM 50:2, NEB)

He chose the tribe of Judah
and Mount Zion which he loved;
He built his sanctuary high as the heavens,
founded like the earth to last for ever.
                   (PSALM 78:68–9, NEB)

Though Jerusalem is also a Holy City, for Christians the concept of the City of God in the New Testatment becomes a more universal vision. It is not tied to a specific place, indeed most of us in England have sung with gusto, "Nor shall my sword sleep in my hand till we have built Jerusalem in England's green and pleasant land."

Jesus' words to the Samaritan woman at the well pointed to a redefinition: "The time is coming when you will worship the Father neither on this mountain (Gerizim), nor in Jerusalem . . . The time approaches, indeed it is already here, when those who are real worshippers will worship the Father in spirit and in truth." (JOHN 4:21–3)

So, though the image of Jerusalem shimmers through the idea of the City of God, it becomes something far wider and refers to the place here and in eternity where God lives and reigns – "the holy dwelling-place of the Most High". So verse 5 – "God is in the midst of her therefore she shall not be moved" referred to Jerusalem at particular times when her survival was threatened, but for Christians it becomes the wonderful reassurance that the City of God is an eternal goal of which we see glimpses in our earthly obedience. The great hymn by John Newton based on words from Psalm 87 expresses the transition to the new vision in Christ:

> Glorious things of thee are spoken
> Zion city of our God! . . .
>
> Saviour, if of Zion's City
> I through grace a member am . . .

It is this vision which restores our hope and faith in the city. It is the faith that where "God is in the midst of her", our city can become the holy dwelling-place of the Most High. We pray every day, "Thy Kingdom come, Thy will be done on earth as it is in heaven", and we are called to serve our city in such a way as the jurisdiction of God is established within the city through footholds and bases, outpourings of spirit and practical love, and the struggle for justice. This has been our agenda in the inner city for many years, and *Faith in the City* was a collage made by the people in the city through the listening ears of the Church. It was a call to the Church and the nation to work for the manifestation of the City of God in our urban scene.

I can and sometimes do feel overwhelmed by the problems facing our city, and there are many times when like Jonah

I would rather run away from the inequalities, the damage to people, the numbers of isolated and alienated, the harshness of the violence in the streets, the inability of people to cope with the size and multiple fragmented sprawl from Dagenham to Denham. But there are so many flashes of sunlight and of joy that the struggle goes on. God is in the midst of her. The City of God is interspersed in our city; there are signs of the divine in every neighbourhood, even the most apparently God-forsaken. So I have come to the point where I go round looking for signs of the Kingdom, where beneath the grime the gold can be seen.

Perhaps it is not surprising that Christian writers express considerable ambivalence about the cities. When *Faith in the City* was being prepared there were those who saw no future. In the book *Theology in the City*[1] which explores some of the theology behind *Faith in the City*, Haddon Wilmer poses these questions about city life: "What kind of goodness can human beings realize? Are human beings one community or many? How near to genuine equality and freedom can we come? . . . Perhaps the city fails to open up a good human possibility. It may show we are caught in a level of human helplessness and structured incompetence." On the other hand, in *The Secular City*[2] Harvey Cox accepted a more positive definition of the city and praised the anonymity, the technology, the communications, the corporate human power in self-assertion and activity. When I read his book in the seventies I scrawled all over it that this was a city for the affluent, for those who had control over their lives, and that it said almost nothing about the millions of people who hang around in cities hoping for a livelihood, searching for a home, existing in a world of fragmented social decay, isolated and alienated from opportunity. To people in control of their lives, London offers great drama, music, art, entertainment, the historical splendour of a capital city, as well as the cosmopolitan bustle of markets and commerce. Yet there is another world of dehumanizing run-down estates of geriatric non-identity, a pornographic subculture, over-crowded tenements, the breakdown of education, the prevalent fear of violence and its spy-hole world. There is a growing tendency amongst the affluent – the heroes and heroines of the advertizers' world, the people in control, like Dives – to make this poor world invisible. In 1989, the Minister for Social Security gave a lecture to show that there was no real poverty in Britain when so many had a television set and a fridge. In a lengthy reappraisal he did not mention homelessness. He did not find it necessary to mention that many people now live in the cardboard boxes which once carried a television set or a fridge. To him they had become invisible. So there are grave doubts and massive questions about the "Secular City".

It is fascinating to read in Harvey Cox's book that he believed the God of the Bible deconsecrated values, disenchanted nature and secularized politics. The dimension of God was so immanent, so within all things, that He became almost indistinguishable from the creation itself. I believe that the Secular City fails precisely because God does not transcend it, because the main refuge and strength is "man come of age": self-reliant, self-sufficient, answerable only to the god within himself, not filled with awe at the enchantment of creation and the consecration of values.

In the last ten years we have been witnesses to a secular

city being built in London's docklands. In the midst of the existing "island" communities is being constructed a new city which the developers hope will thrive if London becomes the capital of Europe. It took many years of battling by the existing communities, by the Churches and the pressure groups, to persuade the developers that "regeneration" was not just a matter of land and buildings but also social regeneration. Though the public relations side of the London Docklands Development Corporation was keen to show a benign face to the local people, the reality behind the smile was strictly commercial. Almost too late they began to realize that it would be in their own self-interest to see the locality as a place for recruitment of the work force. The reason that they did not give time and authority to social regeneration was that corporately they were motivated by a different god. The first people to take the community and social regeneration seriously were the Jewish developers of Canary Wharf. Whether this had its roots in their faith or in their good business sense I don't know, but the social regeneration argument we had been making all along suddenly became fashionable late in the day.

But when we look at Canary Wharf it is difficult to avoid the conclusion that the god being worshipped is Mammon. Prince Charles in his famous TV programme on architecture sat with the architects of Canary Wharf who explained to him that the vast tower blocks were a demonstration of "confidence". His effective reply was to ask, "Confidence in what?" Aye, there's the rub. "Confidence in what?" Where will this new Manhattan find its inspiration? Prince Charles repeatedly used the phrase "the human scale" and he derived this "human" scale from a recognition that we only get human beings and their buildings in proportion when we see them in the perspective of God's scale.

Though the Churches are attempting to help Canary Wharf to work, or rather to ensure that the local community has a share in the opportunity, it is hard for us to be convinced that it bears signs of the City of God. Rather I feel that it is like the Tower of Babel – a monument to man's pride and greed, and I wonder if its fate will be the same. We are facing the question whether we should try to stand for the reality of God in this massive development, or shake the dust off our feet. In the end we come back to the people who will spend their lives there – many of whom will escape home at night to the human scale of their Sussex/Surrey village. We all know that the god who is worshipped in such places as Canary Wharf does not fill the soul of his worshippers. There will be stress and bloodletting and plotting as well as prosperity, ingenuity and glamour – in the rich world of Dallas with its glass towers and lost people.

So where do I look in our city to catch a glimpse of the City of God? I look where people co-operate for the good of the whole, where human beings grow in self-respect and dignity; where the weakest are not made invisible but given special honour; where the splendour of the life God has given us is available not just to the rich; where the scale is such that men and women and children are not dwarfed but allowed to feel they belong to an identifiable community; where the provision in the city is such that there is movement towards equality of opportunity; where there is a bearing of one another's burdens; where people are not oppressed by the guilt deriving from their greed; where the environment gives people defensible space to have their privacy and gives them the opportunity to operate as a community and as a community of communities; where traffic does not destroy them by its noise, dirt and pollution; and where the strong and the wealthy see the poor and work for them for their joint future. I believe that these things depend upon our worshipping God and not Mammon. We only break through to them when the self is put in the proper relationship to God and the sacredness of life is restored. These are the principles which take human form in the glimpses of the City of God that I have seen:

Sitting in the heart of a youth orchestra in the Albert Hall, caught up in their splendour and a trumpet solo played brilliantly by a teenager.

Listening to a young handicapped man confined to a wheelchair describe his new expertize with a computer and praising God for his life.

Learning at the feet of a small Bengali child who held a press conference captivated as she dealt with her homelessness.

Going into a vast Victorian church in the most unpromising part of Hackney and seeing a thousand night-lights shining at the icon of Christ.

Finding a group of businessmen who cared about the local community and modified their plans to include the local people.

Seeing five streams of pilgrims converging of St Paul's Cathedral, bringing gifts for other cities and singing praise to the Lord the Almighty the King of creation.

Speaking with three alcoholics who had been restored to themselves and had found a way of tackling the "great deceiver".

Having thousands of conversations with adults who have been found by God and have allowed Him to turn them round and set them on the Way.

Sharing in a Bible study group in a block of flats where graffiti and fear rule and being able to laugh in the security of Christ.

Opening a new housing project which meets the needs of the elderly and homeless families and seeing their excitement as they moved in.

Appreciating a group who built a hostel for homeless people, which was burnt down twice and on each occasion rebuilt in determination and love.

Seeing a group of children of many races and religions dancing round together without a thought of their racial difference.

Seeing the tall ships moor at Tower Bridge dressed over-all, and all the people from all over the world caught up in it.

Hearing the story of the blitz and sensing the fun and courage which shone in the darkness.

Sitting crammed in a room with colleagues and Christians from Namibia working for their freedom and drawing on their closeness to God.

Above all sharing in the Eucharist with all the truth and beauty and love of it; the hands young and strong, old and frail, manicured and rough-worn — finding those times in the face of all the impossibility when we sing with conviction in our hearts — "Our God reigns".

So many scenes which redeem the time and counter all those other scenes of greed and racism and lust and foul rage, and degrading places, political betrayals and blindness which stain the city and blot out the light.

But this is not just about the signs of an earthly city, though that is our immediate context; it is also about the heavenly city of which these signs are a foretaste. Someone once said that Orthodox worship in Russia provided hope for the people because as they went from the grey streets and grey policies into the splendour and light and mystery of the Orthodox liturgy, they entered a different jurisdiction. Whether it is because of the long battle we have fought in the city or a revelation of God, I do not know, but I have a growing conviction that the most serious damage done to the human psyche by secularism has been to destroy the picture of heaven in people's minds. We must, I believe, rebuild the City of God in our souls. If there is a dimension of God, if we believe the eternal "city" is where God is in His Godness and where angels and archangels and the whole company of heaven have their being, then we have to open our imagination to re-create a view of heaven. It is not enough to locate God in the deep places of our lives, as though God had no transcendent being. The witness of the psalmist is that it is God's dimension which is true and real from eternity. We might do worse than start in humility with the pictures we so easily dismissed in our post-war attempts to be honest to God. Combating literalism was necessary, destroying the picture gallery was not. Our psalm gives us a picture which recurs several times in the Bible: "There is a river whose streams make glad the City of God." Luther transferred the idyll into a mediaeval German town by rendering the verse "Nevertheless shall the city of God remain pleasant and gay with its little fountains." We have other pictures of the River of Life – in Ezekiel 47 where "the spring issues from under the terrace of the temple" and the spring becomes a flood as the beauty and wonder of God flows from His being. The river flowed on and brought life to the trees and even sweetened the foul waters of the Dead Sea. This vision too inspired the writer of the Revelation: "Then he showed me the river of the water of life sparkling like crystal, flowing from the throne of God and of the Lamb down the middle of the city's street." (REVELATION 22:1)

So each friendship, each act of love, each celebration of God, each celebration of life, each act of justice, each act of kindness, each genuine struggle for the common good, are part of the river which flows from the throne of God and of the Lamb. The eternal city shines its glory and its light behind, beyond and through the city we live in. When the city's night and darkness threatens – its size, its alienation, its seedy wickedness – then we trust that "God will help her – and at break of day". As the dawn comes there is a new day to build or restore the damage done.

\* \* \* \* \*

*The nations make uproar and the kingdoms are shaken: but God has lifted his voice and the earth shall tremble.*

Not only was God the only refuge in the upheavals and tumult of nature, but also in the uproar of wars. The God of the Bible is not just the God of individuals, of the pious, but also the God of all nations. The God of Israel is the God of history. His will and purpose are not confined to individual destinies but to the whole corporate existence of mankind. Our contemporary God is often too small — a domestic God — a God who only seems concerned with the personal salvation of individuals; but the God of the Bible is the God of creation and history. The God of the Bible is a mighty God at whose word the universe came to be and at whose word the universe is shaken.

\*  \*  \*  \*  \*

*The Lord of Hosts is with us:*
*the God of Jacob is our stronghold.*

The Lord of Hosts — "Yahweh Sabaoth" sounds trumpets in the mind — the Lord of all nations and of all their history. The great shifts of peoples and nations, conquests and empires are in His hand. It was the amazing vision of the people of Israel that their God Yahweh was the God above all gods — the one true God. The chorus which the people sang in response to the psalm affirmed this majesty over creation and history, and in one of those devastating claims they sang "The God of Jacob is our stronghold." The God whom Jacob encountered in the dream of angels ascending and descending at Bethel, the God whom Jacob wrestled with in the form of a stranger before being reconciled to his brother — this God of a man and then a people was and is the Lord of Hosts.

The God of Jacob reveals to us how absurd the conflict

is between individual and corporate understanding in the political argument of our day. Though Jacob was a man, Jacob was also Israel. The Old Testament calls people to individual obedience and faith, but there is almost no concept of individualism. It is nearly always "we", it is nearly always the people of God, it is nearly always the community. This corporate view emerges and is re-expressed in the New Testament through the new Israel and the second Adam. The City of God and the Body of Christ all talk about interdependence, the community of grace in which individuals must play their part, but which is far greater and more significant in its corporate expression than in its individual members. The God of Jacob, the God of their ancestors, God of history, God of the present, God of the future, is their stronghold. So the chorus affirms the faith of the people of God in response to the declared majesty of God – where God reigns the city endures.

\* \* \* \* \*

*Come then and see what the Lord has done:*
*what destruction he has brought upon the earth.*

We find these words so difficult under the perspective of Christ, the King of Peace. Yet they describe the fate of the nations who make uproar. The Jews had such a faith in God that He was the Lord of history, and they saw the desolation after the storm of war as the direct result of God's judgement. The same destruction can be seen in many countries of the world, but people understand it to be the direct result of the corporate and individual wickedness of the nations rather than the judgement and punishment of

God. There is not such a gap in the interpretation as at first appears. War is the result of enmity with God — enmity with God leads to death and destruction, and so it is the harvest of the misused freedom which God has given us. The psalmist asks us to see in the desolation of war, God's judgement and God's intention to defeat the destructive corporate sin of mankind's aggression.

> *He makes wars to cease in all the world:*
> *he breaks the bow and shatters the spear*
> *and burns the chariots in the fire.*

The vision of peace, given by God, brings hope out of the ruins of the battlefield. God speaks and war will cease, and the weapons of war will be broken up and shattered and the chariots of war burnt. Wherever President Gorbachev's reforms lead us, how many of us believed that East and West would come to monitor each other's destruction of missiles and weapons of war? Yet for a moment the cycle of fear has been broken. Whether the forces of reaction and repression will seal up the dam remains to be seen, yet by Mr Gorbachev's leadership the profound hopes of his people for peace and freedom from slavery and warmongery have been released. Isaiah looked to the most unexpected source in the alien conqueror to see hope for Israel — "Here is Cyrus, my anointed" (ISAIAH 45:1) How do we know that President Gorbachev is the result of secular accidents? Maybe the prayers of Russian Orthodox grandmothers, of Latvian and Estonian dissidents and martyrs, have been God's agents in preparing the way of the Lord.

\* \* \* \* \*

*Be still and know that I am God.*

In the tumult of history, as we stagger beneath the implications of the majesty of God and His greatness, beyond our understanding, the psalmist calls us to silence and to know God Himself. We small dots on the canvas are reminded that we are not insignificant, we are not useless or helpless; because we can begin to rediscover the kingdom of God we can enter the eternal City − now, as we remain silent with God who joins His spirit to our longing: "Be still and know that I am God." This is the place where we are with Him and He with us. This is the place where, in a marvellous affirmation of power and vision of the future kingdom, the Lord says:

> *I will be exalted among the nations,*
> *I will be exalted upon the earth.*

So we respond again with the chorus in assurance of faith;

> *The Lord of Hosts is with us:*
> *The God of Jacob is our stronghold.*

# PSALM 51
## Have Mercy on Me,
## O God

*Have mercy on me O God in your enduring goodness:*
*according to the fulness of your compassion*
    *blot out my offences.*

*Wash me throughly from my wickedness:*
*and cleanse me from my sin.*

*For I acknowledge my rebellion:*
*and my sin is ever before me.*

*Against you only have I sinned*
    *and done what is evil in your eyes:*
*so you will be just in your sentence*
    *and blameless in your judging.*

*Surely in wickedness I was brought to birth:*
*and in sin my mother conceived me.*

*You that desire truth in the inward parts:*
*O teach me wisdom in the secret places of the heart.*

*Purge me with hyssop and I shall be clean:*
*wash me and I shall be whiter than snow.*

*Make me hear of joy and gladness:*
*let the bones which you have broken rejoice.*

*Hide your face from my sins:*
*and blot out all my iniquities.*

*Create in me a clean heart O God:*
*and renew a right spirit within me.*

*Do not cast me out from your presence:*
*do not take your holy spirit from me.*

*O give me the gladness of your help again:*
*and support me with a willing spirit.*

*Then will I teach transgressors your ways:*
*and sinners shall turn to you again.*

*O Lord God of my salvation, deliver me from bloodshed:*
*and my tongue shall sing of your righteousness.*

*O Lord open my lips:*
*and my mouth shall proclaim your praise.*

*You take no pleasure in sacrifice or I would give it:*
*burnt-offerings you do not want.*

*The sacrifice of God is a broken spirit:*
*a broken and contrite heart O God you will not despise.*

*In your graciousness do good to Zion:*
*rebuild the walls of Jerusalem.*

*Then will you delight in right sacrifices*
*in burnt-offerings and oblations:*
*then will they offer young bulls upon your altar.*

This is a tough psalm. The writer explores the unacceptable
area of his life and the need for forgiveness and restoration.
It is always depressing to concentrate on our sins, yet it is
no good pretending we don't do them or that they will go

away if we ignore the self which does them. We go to the doctor to find out what is wrong with us, hoping that there is a single easily-remedied cause, but we know that we are all vulnerable to chronic and fatal diseases. We need to know the truth — even if we don't want to — and we need to start the treatment as soon as possible. Our aim is to get better, to be made whole. And so it is with this psalm. It asks awkward questions and does not hesitate to deal out the treatment. It does not just look at symptoms but at underlying causes. In the end, however, it is a source of hope, because it carries the promise that if we accept the treatment we shall be healed. This psalm again leads to Christ and what he did for us in bearing the sins of the world, and washing us clean.

\* \* \* \* \*

*Have mercy on me O God in your enduring goodness:*
*according to the fulness of your compassion*
*blot out my offences.*

"Ask for mercy" is one thing "real" men will not do. When beaten at school, bullied in the back streets, imprisoned in war, in fights after drinking, to "ask for mercy" would be to admit our weakness, to recognize that we are defeated and to put ourselves wholly in the debt of our opponent. "Mercy" is a big downward-looking word which any self-respecting person with an ounce of proper pride would not want. It is, in the contemporary scene, a word used by the soft, the feeble, the defeated. It conveys to contemporary people precisely the fawning submission which they so dislike in religion.

The longing for mercy is central to the expression of our Christian and Jewish faiths, as well as to the other great theistic faiths of our world. Our liturgy often repeats the theme:

> Lord, have mercy upon us.
> Christ, have mercy upon us.
> Lord, have mercy upon us.

Our words of forgiveness are these:

> Almighty God,
> who forgives all who truly repent,
> have mercy upon you.

In this word "mercy" we can see clearly the contrast between belief and unbelief. Coming to faith demonstrates a fundamental change from the self-assertion, self-sufficiency and human-centred creed, to the recognition that our lives are lived out before an Almighty God who is beyond our understanding and our imagination. To say and believe "Have mercy on me, O God", does not involve the least lessening of the self. When we witness the immensity of a storm or see the profound ocean or guess at the scope of space, we do not experience a reduction of the self. There is the mixture of awe and thankfulness and exhilaration as our inner selves open and expand towards the wonder of God.

"Mercy" in contemporary language suggests submission to an enemy who drives us in the end to beg, and this is totally different from the mercy of God, who reaches towards us with all the mysteries and secrets of the universe in His mind, and in His majestic and tender love. When we realize the otherness of God, as we gaze upon Him, we are bound to say, "Have mercy on me O God in your everlasting goodness." To place myself in the mercy of God is to rediscover the freedom I have lost by my absurd egoism. To discover the perspective of God helps me to fit into the landscape, and to restore my sense of proportion. But above all, "Have mercy upon me O God ..." expresses my yearning to be in God, with God and through God, where eternally I shall find my peace. The effect of this repeated "have mercy on me" is to create an attitude of realistic and healthy submission to the Creator of all universes, whose chief characteristic is steadfast love.

St Augustine assumed that this psalm was written by David, and so his interpretation is based on the penitence of David after he had stolen Bathsheba and caused her husband to be killed in battle; but, as I have pointed out earlier, it is impossible to establish whether or not any one of the psalms refers to any particular person or situation.

As we see many times in the psalms, the vision of the goodness and love of God leads immediately to the need for forgiveness and the cry for mercy.

> *According to the fulness of your compassion*
> *blot out my offences.*

The word translated "compassion" suggests the tenderness of a mother who understands only too well the struggles and weaknesses of her child, as we see so beautifully expressed in Hosea, describing the love of God for Israel:

> It was I who taught them to walk,
> I who had taken them in my arms;

but they did not know that I harnessed them in
  leading-strings
  and led them with bonds of love –
that I had lifted them like a little child to my cheek,
  that I had bent down to feed them.

(HOSEA 11:3–4)

This is not the spoiling of the besotted mother who possesses her child and indulges him, but the mother who understands, yet in her heart most wants her child to grow to be a person in their own right. The word "compassion" is important for the Christian too. What the Jew believes about the steadfast love and compassion of God has been demonstrated for the Christian in the life and experience of Jesus. It is on that basis – that God is able to sympathize, feel with, have compassion on us – that we approach Him.

"In the days of his earthly life he offered up prayers and petitions, with loud cries and tears" (HEBREWS 5:7). Because of the human experience of Jesus taken into God we approach a Lord who knows from within the narrow confinement of a human life, what it is to struggle from the womb to the grave. "For ours is not a high priest unable to sympathize with our weaknesses, but one who, because of his likeness to us, has been tested every way, only without sin" (HEBREWS 4:15). However great and unreachable and unimaginable God may seem, the bridge has been made, and the compassion of God has a human dimension through the being of Christ.

Verse 1 of Psalm 51 continues, "Blot out my offences." Weiser, in his commentary, points us to Exodus 32:32: "Blot out my name, I pray, from thy book which thou hast

120

written", and Psalm 69:30 (ASB), where the reverse image
is used: "Let them be blotted out from the book of the
living." The idea recurs that there is a record kept of our
sins and misdemeanours as well as the book of life in which
are recorded the names of the righteous.

I hope to God that He does not keep a record of our
offences — even though we ourselves do! We are made up
of our past. Our goodness and badness are stored in our
computer. It disturbs me how easily I can bring to mind
the things of which I am ashamed. It only needs someone
we know to die, to parade before our inner eye all our
failures and hurts which we perpetrated against them. The
person has died and we cannot now put right all the wrongs
we did. Sudden death can leave everyone in a state of guilt
with no time to mend the broken relationships, to blot out
the hurtful past. It is also true that our past can drag us
down, by persuading us that we can never change, but are
in a strait-jacket of patterned and addictive reactions. How
do we change a pattern of hate, or lust, or greed, if we have
to carry within us the repeated failures and weaknesses?
In our weakness, our failures can seem so much more
ourselves than the good we have done, the love we have
shown, the generosity we have expressed.

In the film *The Mission*, a mercenary slave trader is brought
to penitence by his Jesuit friend. He is unable to forgive
himself for the acts of murder and slavery which he has
committed. The priest and his penitent set out to climb to
the mountain where the Indians, who had been his victims,
live. In his desire to punish himself, the mercenary ties a
huge bundle of armour and weapons he had used in his
evil days to himself by a rope. He carries this impossible

load up the cliff face, and when the priest thinks he has done enough he tries to free him. But the mercenary is still not ready to receive forgiveness and to blot out his wickedness recorded — engraved — on his own mind. After harrowing struggles, they reach the top of the escarpment and the penitent, covered with mud and sores, slumps to the ground. The Indians come out of the forest. On seeing and knowing him, one of their number goes up to the penitent with a knife and it looks as though he is going to slit his throat — which would release him from his guilt — but instead he cuts the rope and the burden crashes down the hillside and the penitent is free, laughing and crying at once. His sins are blotted out in such a way that he could receive the forgiveness pronounced by the Indian.

There are so many of us who believe in theory that God has wiped the slate clean and torn up the pages of our book, but who cannot take that forgiveness into our hearts where we could laugh and cry with relief that we were free. The self-accusation is sometimes so deeply written into our character that we cannot believe the good news that we are loved and forgiven. For such a person the moment when he or she accepts the truth is the moment of conversion. It is the Amazing Grace promised to all who believe. But even then the old scars of guilt still hurt sometimes, and we have to push the path of pain aside in the name of Christ who has set us free. For those who never seem to find assurance of forgiveness until they see it in God in heaven, we can only stand by in the hope and freedom we have known, not to further stimulate their sense of guilt but to see them as loved and forgiven children of God who will one day smile in Him.

\* \* \* \* \*

*Wash me thoroughly from my wickedness:*
*and cleanse me from my sin.*

In the familiar double statement of a thought there is a richness "Wash me thoroughly" (somehow the Prayer Book word "throughly" said much more) suggests the washing of clothes at the river, with the scrubbing and pounding to get out the stains. The cleansing suggests a healing which begins inside us. Why should a particular person make me so angry? Why do I have so little self-control? Why do I have these dreadful feelings of envy and resentment? The answers lie in our nature and the choices we have made — that mixture of what we are because we are human, and what we have become because of what we have thought and done. So we achieve our personality by the working of our experience upon our nature. This is why the cleansing and the washing have to act upon us thoroughly to bathe our intellect, our emotions and our whole being. Our baptism should be the time when we wash away the stains, when we die to the old self, when we are made new. This comes across more strongly in baptism by total immersion, symbolizing the uncompromising whole-heartedness of the sacrament as we go through the waters of the Red Sea, die, and rise again with Christ. In this sense we can be baptized again and again because every time we come to the Lord asking to be washed and cleansed we are submitting ourselves to the only process (that is, the forgiveness of God) which can restore to us our well-being. I think of a shore covered with all the rubbish and debris of the day, washed clean and restored by the night tide. This is the vision expressed with such beauty by Edwin Muir in his poem "Transfiguration":

## The Lord's Song

So from the ground we felt that virtue branch
Through all our veins till we were whole, our wrists
As fresh and pure as water from a well,
Our hands made new to handle holy things,
The source of all our seeing rinsed and cleansed
Till earth and light and water entering there
Gave back to us the clear unfallen world.
We would have thrown away our clothes for
   lightness,
But that even they, though sour and travel stained,
Seemed, like our flesh, made of immortal substance,
And the soiled flax and wool lay light upon us
Like friendly wonders, flower and flock entwined
As in a morning field.

. . .

The shepherds' hovels shone, for underneath
The soot we saw the stone clean at the heart
As on the starting day. The refuse heaps
Were grained with that fine dust that made the
   world;
For he had said, "To the pure all things are pure."
And when we went into the town, he with us,
The lurkers under doorways, murderers,
With rags tied round their feet for silence, came
Out of themselves to us and were with us,
And those who hide within the labyrinth
Of their own loneliness and greatness came,
And those entangled in their own devices,
The silent and the garrulous liars, all
Stepped out of their dungeons and were free.[1]

\*   \*   \*   \*   \*

*For I acknowledge my rebellion:*
*and my sin is ever before me*

"I acknowledge my rebellion" — that is the difficult part. How do we come to recognize that we have set ourselves against the will of God? We can be so caught up in our own interpretation of our lives. How often we hear ourselves and others repeating over and over again our self-righteous stories. It is a tough shell to crack. We charge along, convinced that we are in the right, that we are more sinned against than sinning, and don't know how to be sorry. The people of God, according to the Bible, are especially prone to being a rebellious, stiff-necked people. They only seem to see their own rebellion for what it is by being broken and reduced to nothing. Like the Prodigal Son, it is not until we realize we are lost and empty and hungry that we have the sense to see that we have rebelled against our Father. But once the rebellion is acknowledged, release is near at hand. The father came out to meet his son and loved and embraced him. The battle was won when the rebellion was acknowledged. St Paul lived his holy pre-Christ life, tensed up and fighting to be good with all his own strength. When he finally encountered Christ, the words he heard were, "Saul, Saul, why do you persecute me? It is hard for you, this kicking against the goad" (ACTS 26:14). It is hard to rebel. Whatever form it takes for us, rebellion against God brings unhappiness and undermines the integrity of our life. In the same way, recognition of our guilt can open us up to peace, relief and a restored energy.

"My sin is ever before me." There are those who say that this means that we are always approaching our next sin. Our

problem is that we cannot see it looming up. We cannot bring
into our minds sufficient sense of the misery it will cause,
to stop us doing it. Though that seems to be true, I do not
think it is what the psalmist means. The Hebrew word
"*Nesed*" suggests that the Cambridge Commentary is right
in translating this phrase "my sins confront me all day long".
This appears to reflect a rather morbid concentration upon
our sins, almost a self-indulgent obsession which helps no one.

There is a rightness about the rhythm of a daily confession
at morning and evening time with a robust living of our
lives in between. Some of the most hurtful things we do,
we never learn about or only discover at a later date. As
a man and as a bishop, I hardly dare contemplate the
number of times I have said something hurtful, or failed
someone who was relying on me, and not even known. The
things I know about are bad enough, let alone the faults
which are a secret even from me. Our sins do accuse us,
but we live under grace, and when we come to the judgement
seat the Holy Spirit stands by us and speaks in our defence.
The psalm seems to point to Christ who stood in the dock
on our behalf and then became the Advocate to plead for
us in our daily confrontation with our sin. We are not the
right advocates for ourselves, not only because our sin is
ever before us, but also because, as St Augustine pointed
out: "Thou engagest thyself as defender of thy sin, thou art
conquered: no innocent patron hast thou engaged . . ."[2]

\* \* \* \* \*

*Against you only have I sinned.*

It would be impossible to say this if it meant that we were

blameless as far as our fellow human beings were concerned. But we can understand it if it means that all sin is an offence against God, so that to hurt or damage or fail our neighbour is to hurt or damage or fail God. This is another of those dividing places which separate believers from unbelievers. For the person who does not recognize there is God, the only offence can be against the self of other human beings, but for the believer there is the whole realm of sin against God, which can be a matter of personal attitude or conviction, which can be the content of our secret thoughts, which can be the failures in our direct relationship with God Himself.

\* \* \* \* \*

*(I have) done what is evil in your eyes*

It is one of the sources of pain in the life of faith that we never seem to reach our goal. Whenever – if ever – we tackle our most obvious sins, behind them there are still the higher peaks of love to be scaled: "You have learned that they were told, 'Do not commit adultery.' But what I tell you is this: If a man looks on a woman with a lustful eye, he has already committed adultery with her in his heart." (MATTHEW 5:27–8) The journey inwards keeps on unpeeling new layers. For instance, if we were to analyse violence we might say that its seed lies in resentment and anger, but behind the resentment and anger lies the prejudice, and behind the prejudice lies the lack of respect, behind the lack of respect lies the lack of proper self-love . . . So the journey with God keeps going deeper and deeper into the motives and causes. Doing what is evil in God's eyes is to be exposed to the intense light of God's love the nearer we come to the vison of God Himself.

\* \* \* \* \*

*So you will be just in your sentence*
*and blameless in your judging.*

We will know only too well how right He was and is, and yet: ". . . in making all mankind prisoners to disobedience, God's purpose was to show mercy to all mankind. O depth of wealth, wisdom, and knowledge in God! How unsearchable his judgements, how untraceable his ways!" (ROMANS 11:32–3)

The psalmist's picture of the judgement of God draws out an exclamation – almost a shout – of anxiety. St Augustine was only too aware of the awesome righteousness of God. He was able to contemplate the judgement of God without despair only because of the great mercy of God. "Thou wilt not be able to take away from the Lord God His justice: entreat mercy, but observe the justice."[3] Somehow in the mercy of God what was forgiven was no longer ascribed to the sinner. In Christ, justice was preserved because He carried the sins of the world, like a universal scapegoat. In His love for us and in His innocence He paid the price, and so reconciled us to the God of justice. In this way, Christ frees us from that which has been forgiven in the mercy and truth of God. It is a hard doctrine to swallow, but it is food and drink to those who see that the death of Christ was not an unjust substitution, but a demonstration of wonderful love, which goes right to the heart of our own feelings of helplessness.

\* \* \* \* \*

## Psalm 51

*Surely in wickedness I was brought to birth
and in sin my mother conceived me.*

This verse has been used to suggest that sexual intercourse is sinful, that mankind is infected at birth, that although innocent, the new born baby is in need of immediate baptism to save it from hell and damnation which would be the just reward of original sin. But its meaning is quite different and more understandable. It refers to the human condition as described in the story of Adam. Adam was not a particular person in history, but he represents the coming to birth of the human race. His story is, in a sense, true of all of us. He fell from his innocent harmony and happiness with God through his disobedience and his attempt to make himself like God. This is the myth which describes the key to our human alienation, and it is in this condition that we are all born. Hence "in wickedness was I brought to birth."

Each generation sees in the text what it is ready to see and often what it wants to see – and we are no different. There is a truth in the saying that in our very humanness we are prone to aggression and greed, etc. It is also true that the story of Adam is the story of everyone, because we are all attracted by the idea of rebellion against God. There is a boy aged fourteen who lives near us and is constantly in trouble with the neighbours and with the police. He has no remorse, he appears at this early age to have killed off any moral sense in himself. He has never known what it is like to be able to trust someone. The blows dealt to him by his personal environment have made him almost a savage. Lawlessness has become his way of life. I see in him an extreme parable of us all; we are all born and have to live our lives in a human environment riddled with wickedness, past and present. I was born into the British heritage with its good and its evil, into a city with its reservoir of good and evil, into a family with its strengths and weaknesses, its love and its deception. The moment Adam takes the fruit of the tree of the knowledge of good and evil he is separated from God and has to live with the disturbance, the frustration and guilt of that separation. It is into that experience and that world that we are born.

In our relationship with our parents, too, there are a whole range of feelings and actions which fall short of the love of God. We are in part the product of our relationship with our father and mother. In all these senses we are born into a sinful world and a sinful environment. But, thanks be to God, for many of us there is the great countervailing force of loving affection, of trust and security, of good example and total support. It is the tragedy of those children/adults who almost never receive such affirmation that they most often become overburdened by their potential wickedness. But St Augustine reminds us that, though our personality is wounded, the possibility of healing remains: ". . . if any that hath already fallen heareth these words, and that hath in his conscience any evil thing . . . let him heed the greatness of the wound, but not despair of the majesty of the Physician."[4] However much we feel we have inflicted wounds upon ourselves, we can always turn back to the forgiveness of God. "If from thee sin could not be excluded, be not hope of pardon excluded."[5] However deep the self-inflicted wound, the healing was great enough. But our penance and our determination to change are costly. "(God) smiteth the rottenness of the deed, He healeth the pain of the wound. Physicians (surgeons!) do this when they cut, they smite and heal."[6]

\*   \*   \*   \*   \*

*You that desire truth in the inward parts:*
*O teach me wisdom in the secret places of the heart.*

It is the test of our determination to find God that we set our minds and hearts on finding God's truth. In the very rules we make for our conversation with God are sown the seeds of truth or self-deception. It is amazing how far into ourselves can go our defences against the truth. We try to paint religion on our faces like a clown uses make-up, when the citadel within us is still locked and unexplored. It has been a sadness to me to see how far we who engage in daily prayer for a lifetime can keep our own motives concealed from ourselves. Religion which does not storm the innermost citadel and which does not allow the truth to work in the secret places of the heart is not safe. It is a form of neurosis which is afraid to expose the whole of the self to the love of God. So the spiritual journey should be a journey towards honesty about the self to ourselves, and an openness through that, to the truth which God imparts.

Again the psalmist recognizes the need for inner cleansing, makes his prayer to God:

*Purge me with hyssop and I shall be clean:*
*wash me and I shall be whiter than snow.*

As A. A. Anderson says, "A bunch of hyssop was used at the first Passover for the sprinkling of the lintels and doorposts of Hebrew houses; in later times it was used in the cleansing of the leper as well as in the purification of one defiled by contact with a corpse."[7] It is difficult for us to get inside the idea of ritual uncleanness which was so basic to the Old Testament believers. We know what it is like to shudder in contact with evil, but we do not feel or understand that a cripple or a menstruating woman or a damaged organ could be thought of as "unclean". It is as though this sense of ritual uncleanness has died in us and cannot be re-created. This does not stop a similar basic feeling of offence emerging in wrong ways, such as the rejection of homosexual people, or a sense of distaste for people of other races, or our fear and abhorrence at severe abnormality. This is not to say that there are no proper taboos, but they have to be re-examined in the light of experience. The psalmist is able to appeal to the shudder caused by the leper, or anything unclean, and recognize that God alone can restore purity and wholeness, so that he will be washed whiter than snow. St Augustine says in one of his parables that the hyssop adheres to the rock by its roots . . . "Do thou also take hold, with the root of thy love, on thy Rock."[8]

\* \* \* \* \*

*Make me hear of joy and gladness*
*let the bones which you have broken rejoice.*

In just a few words we come up against a far-reaching issue of life and faith: "Let the bones which you have broken rejoice." We are plunged here into what Harry Williams called the wilderness. How many times in the Christian life we experience a sort of disintegration where it feels as though we are broken. I have known the near despair that I have recognized in others, and which perhaps we share with our Lord ("My heart is ready to break with grief", Mark 14:34). I have experienced it both in the feeling of helplessness in my battles with myself and also in the many defeats in my battles in the world. For the Jew it is contained in the opening words of Psalm 22:

> My God, my God why have you forsaken me:
> Why are you so far from helping me
> and from the words of my groaning?

For the Christian it is in those same words cried out from the Cross.

"The bones" in the text make it clear that it is our whole human being which is broken and then restored. The Old Testament never lets us get away with dividing up body, mind and spirit. It totally affirms what is called the holistic approach to healing – that is, the recognition that we are a unity of body, mind and spirit, and therefore healing often requires action in all these facets of a person. Thank God the Christian faith rejected the idea that somehow at death our soul escaped from our body. Because of the risen body of Christ, the Church came to the vision of the resurrection as the whole self being raised and re-created. Most of us experience this unity of bones and spirit when we have toothache or when our stress and anxiety create real pain, which hurts even if people insist on calling it psychosomatic. We also know that a mild depression can affect our whole system and make us feel physically down, and our feeling physically down can make us depressed. We can all recognize such experiences and know that, with all our complexity, we are also a unity.

"The bones which you have broken . . ." At one level this is a scandalous thing to say. It is as though God brings our personality to breakdown. It is certainly true that people see God's hand in our tragic experiences through living in the risky, dangerous, accidental world. Although God is accountable for the whole creation, the arena necessary for our freedom is an insurer's nightmare. I do not believe that God causes multiple sclerosis or cancer, except in so far as they are expressions of the incredible living organism which made life possible. Nor do I believe that God arranges for a tyre to burst and plunge a car across the path of the on coming traffic. This is all part of our accident-prone life. When we come up against such tragic happenings it is hard to see that the terrible ambiguity is necessary to the human experience of freedom. I cannot love unless I can hate, I cannot live unless I can die, I cannot be brave unless there is danger, I cannot grow unless there is decay. God has created and allowed and is therefore responsible for the pain and the freedom.

On the other hand, I do believe that disciples are quite often taken to pieces and put back together again. It can be that in our journey with God we have built on wrong foundations, and as a result our whole building is unstable. I knew a priest who after many years found the whole church experience empty and it left him play-acting at the altar. He experienced a breakdown, and only slowly was he able to build on firmer foundations, having been profoundly disillusioned. Many of us go through similar experiences, if not as severe as that. In this sense God is seen to be drawing us to Himself, and He knows that there are changes that can only be made through fire, that until our idolatrous system breaks — the false neurotic framework we have built for our "safety" — the new person cannot be created. Then we can say "the bones which you have broken". It is also true that people are able to discover, through the terrible accidents and tragedies of life, a new strength and vision — like Ronnie, whom I confirmed three days before he died of AIDS, who told us that although he had become blind he did not need his eyes to see what God wanted him to see; or like the Christian blind woman who would not pray to recover her sight because she would not be able to teach the blind so well. There are a multitude of ways in which people come to terms with the traumas of life and find through them a new and deeper relationship with God. In a way, God is powerless in an accidental and cruel world, and yet, as Christ showed on the cross, He has the real and ultimate spiritual power which can transform failure, breakdown and defeat into a very special victory.

"Make me hear of joy and gladness . . . let the bones which you have broken rejoice." Whilst we are broken we are usually blind to the possibility of restoration. Others may see it, but we cannot. For us there is only the desolation and the being caught in our own hurt and self-pity. But, by a transformation that seems to spring from places too deep for us to know, the purpose begins to appear, the grief is released and the relationship with the self and with God is restored. When this has happened several times, we begin to see it as God's way of rebuilding us, and we come to see that joy does come in the morning time, that what seemed unfathomable loneliness was for a purpose. Indeed, such experience can be seen as part of the creative purpose whereby an evil is shifted, some progress towards the Kingdom of God is made. If the agony of Christ in the garden saved mankind, then our lesser agonies can achieve lesser but important goals.

My favourite story of the struggle involved in restoration is the experience of Jacob before his encounter with Esau his brother whom he had wronged so badly. The night before meeting his brother again after many years, he spent alone by the river Jabbok and "a man wrestled with him there till daybreak. When the man saw that he could not throw Jacob, he struck him in the hollow of his thigh, so that Jacob's hip was dislocated as they wrestled" (GENESIS 32:24–5). Jacob demanded the man's blessing. "Jacob called the place Peniel, 'because,' he said, 'I have seen God face to face' " (v 30). At dawn Jacob longed to see his brother who "ran to meet him and embraced him". The struggling in prayer with God led to the reconciliation with his brother. Many people who follow Christ or take the service of God seriously learn the cost of reconciliation, of new hope, of salvation, and discover the greatness of the joy which follows the storm. In so many experiences of my life I have only discovered the purpose and the meaning of my struggles at some later time and in another place. It did not stop Jesus crying, "Take this cup away from me" (LUKE 22:42), and how much less will it stop us wishing that we would never be broken again, whatever the joy we discovered when the sun came out.

### Hide your face from my sins

It is strange how when an adult cries we want to look away,

to avoid their and our embarrassment. The number of times I have been with someone who begins to have the much-needed weep and I find myself looking down or aside. We also often try to hide our tears from other people – making sure our eyes are dry. "Will anyone know I have been crying?" If we feel like that about health-giving, justifiable tears, what must it be like to have God looking at us in our shame? It is difficult enough coping with the thought that a human being we love can see us at our worst, but how much worse to be under the eyes of God. So this prayer comes from the heart.

> *Create in me a clean heart O God:*
> *and renew a right spirit within me.*

I once spent an afternoon in the crypt of Christ Church Spitalfields with the alcoholics who were there, and so powerful was my experience of indentifying with them that on the following Sunday I said this in a broadcast:

> As I sat and talked with them, I felt pity for them in their struggle, yet knew that they have to be tough on themselves and need hard advice. I did not feel superior to them, although their lives had plunged into the pit. Quite the reverse – perhaps to God I look like the alcoholic. He knows that I keep on trying to conquer my weakness. He is always reaching out to me and offering the strength I need – but somehow, at key moments I turn my back on His help. But the wonder of it is that God keeps on taking me back, wiping the slate clean and giving me yet another new start . . . That's what the bishop and the alcoholic have in common – we both depend upon the

endless patience of God and find the strength we need from faith in God and His trust in us.[9]

St Augustine tells again the story of the woman taken in adultery, who was brought before Jesus by her accusers who wanted to stone her to death. He said the famous words "Let him who is without sin throw the first stone," and they all went away, one by one. When they had all retreated, Augustine says, "Remained the adulteress and the Lord; remained she wounded and He Physician; remained the great misery and the great mercy."[10]

Weiser, in his commentary on the Psalms, speaks of "The impossibility of self-conquest". At the end of St Paul's struggles to keep the holy law, to achieve holiness, he found himself in despair bcause everyone falls short of the ideal, and indeed all who strive to be good know from their own experience the agony he expressed in his famous words which have saved me on many occasions: "For though the will to do good is there, the deed is not. The good which I want to do, I fail to do; but what I do is the wrong which is against my will." (ROMANS 7:18–19)

This recognition of our inability to save ourselves is expressed in the psalmist's plea to God – "Create in me a new heart." He recognized that our fallen nature needed a new act of remaking by God to find the wholeness we desire.

The time is coming, says the Lord, when I will make a new covenant with Israel and Judah. It will not be like the covenant I made with their forefathers when I took them by the hand and led them out of Egypt. Although they broke my covenant, I was patient with them, says the Lord. But this is the covenant which I will make with Israel after those days, says the Lord; I will set my law within them and write it on their hearts; I will become their God and they shall become my people. (JEREMIAH 31:31-3)

The old covenant of the law of God set on stone tablets had failed and a new initiative of God was needed to write the law upon their hearts. The new relationship was one in which the people would be open to God, and in that fusion of God and man there would be a rebirth.

Ezekiel, too, confronted with the disobedience and idolatry of the people, recognized that it needed some profound new activity of God in His love to change the very hearts of the people:

I will give them a different heart and put a new spirit into them; I will take the heart of stone out of their bodies and give them a heart of flesh. Then they will conform to my statutes and keep my laws. They will become my people, and I will become their God. (EZEKIEL 11:19-20)

To those who practise Judaism and Christianity, these words are so familiar that we can miss their fundamental radical nature. The Law had a purpose — namely to face mankind with the righteous demands of God — demands which were for our well-being. To obey was to live more abundantly. But mankind has to face up to the failure of the "law" to change the heart, and so the result is our dependence upon the initiative and grace of God. Although we are called to be obedient, yet in the end the obedience is a gift. If we take a familiar example: we can be shown that smoking can and does kill us, and that it damages other people. This education confronts us with the wrong in what we are doing and, in some cases, where the heart is ready to receive "the law", the change may follow. But for many of us, the facts, the distressing results of smoking, are not enough to change our behaviour. The same could be said of drink and drugs and lust and greed, etc., etc. Our will-power is the first resource we draw upon, and indeed it is unlikely that a "cure" will be achieved without a considerable exercise of our will, yet for many of us — in many situations — we betray ourselves again, and we learn that there is need of God-given grace to transform us. When we allow the Spirit of God to join with our spirit, we can glimpse a possible victory. The drag of established patterns of behaviour can still be overwhelming through so many self-inflicted wounds, and yet there is hope through Christ Jesus alive in us. So we need never lose our belief in our God-given ability to change. Although we shall often fear that we have lost the battle, we return to the promise of God that He can create in us a clean heart and put a new Spirit within us.

This is something that the contemporary age does not understand. We seem to lurch between two contrasted fashions. On the one hand there is the permissive approach which appears to assure us that if we pursue whatever experiences we want, we shall learn and arrive at our proper maturity. On the other, it is the claim of the "Victorian" parent that duty and punishment achieve goodness and righteousness. So we swing from the "I am what I am" school to the "You will be what I tell you and woe betide you if you don't" school. These ideas emerge in social attitudes not only in schools but in public responses to poverty, to unemployment and to failure. On the one hand, the afflicted person is deemed unable to help him or herself, and he or she has the right to almost any self-expression of the anger and resentment, or on the other the poor are told to pull themselves together, to snap out of their self-pity, to stand on their own feet. The arguments over the Welfare State seem to me to derive from this inadequate analysis of the human condition. But if we were to attend to the Christian understanding, we would discover that both are aspects of the truth. There is manifestly no excuse for opting out of our own responsiblity for being ourselves. We may not mug other people, nor act in an anarchic way to damage the people around us, because we are hard done by. People who live in infinitely worse conditions than we do, often demonstrate marvellous spiritual virtues. We may not say, "It's not our fault and therefore we do whatever we like", because it is in claiming our responsibility for ourselves that we become a person. On the other hand, many factors in life threaten to overwhelm and destroy people – severe disability, long-term unemployment, homelessness, disturbed or non-existent family life – and the victory over such handicaps ultimately lies in the love of God. It is the duty of society to reflect that love in its way of operating and its care for the poor. It is God who creates a new heart in the individual and in society, but each of us and our corporate action has to take responsibility for ourselves and our neighbour. God's demand leads to the recognition that we need Grace, and the Grace of God raises in our hearts the demand

\* \* \* \* \*

*Do not cast me out from your presence:*
*do not take your holy spirit from me.*

Though the Spirit blows through the Old Testament, the expression 'holy spirit' occurs only here and in Isaiah 63:10 – 11, where it expresses both the person of God and the activity of God. Here the psalmist uses the expression to describe the indwelling of God, which could not be claimed as fixed and final, but rather was a gift upon which the psalmist depended. "Do not cast me out from your presence" is developed and re-expressed in terms of a plea that God would not take away the Holy Spirit. For God to take away His Spirit would be to plunge the person into despair, and expose them to the assaults of the evil and malign spirits of the universe.

In the story of King Saul can be seen the man chosen by God for a special purpose, inspired by the Spirit, but then the Spirit of God left him and an evil spirit rushed upon him and he raved in his house. "The spirit of the Lord had forsaken Saul, and at times an evil spirit from the Lord would seize him suddenly" (1 Samuel 16:14). So he went from bad to worse and he became consumed with envy of David, as he saw David's love for Jonathan and his popularity with the people. This vivid picture of the relationship of God with Saul, through the gift of His Spirit and the desperate effects of his loss of God, give a picture of the passion behind the plea in this verse. It was through God's breath (spirit) that man became a living being, and to take that spirit away was to consign a person to despair and death.

For the Christian, the wonderful vision of the indwelling Spirit of God in St John's Gospel and in St Paul's letters gives a new and profound expression to this prayer of the psalmist, because the Holy Spirit is characterized by Christ. When we pray for the gift of the Holy Spirit, we are not inviting the God known only on awesome Sinai, the Almighty, the creator of the universe, but also we are welcoming the love of that God as expressed in a very human person, Jesus. The writer to the Hebrews marks out for us this transformation of our religion:

> Remember where you stand: not before the palpable, blazing fire of Sinai, with the darkness, gloom, and whirlwind, the trumpet-blast and the oracular voice, which they heard, and begged to hear no more; for they could not bear the command, "If even an animal touches the mountain, it must be stoned." So appalling was the sight that Moses said, "I shudder with fear."

> No, you stand before Mount Zion and the city of the living God, heavenly Jerusalem, before myriads of angels, the full concourse and assembly of the first-born citizens of heaven, and God the judge of all, and the spirits of good men made perfect, and Jesus the mediator of a new covenant, whose sprinkled blood has better things to tell than the blood of Abel. (HEBREWS 12:18–24)

St John records that Jesus promised that He and the Father would come and make their home in those who loved Him. He said, "Anyone who loves me will heed what I say; then my Father will love him, and we will come to him and make our dwelling with him" (John 14:23). Throughout the last conversations Jesus had with His disciples, He talked about the gifts of the Spirit – a Spirit of truth, a counsellor, the active love of God in the believer's life.

St Paul described this Spirit as joining with our spirit and thus enabling us to pray. When we cry "Father" to God, His Spirit is already at work in us. The Spirit working in us helps us defeat the negative, damaging and sinful sides of our lives, and grows within our personality a harvest of those most holy and divine virtues which express the liberty and splendour of the children of God. Our bodies, said St Paul, are temples of the Holy Spirit calling us to reverence – as in the Temple – for the presence of God within us. The Spirit also is the encourager, the one who strengthens the sinews of the soul, who selects and sorts out and mobilizes the good in us, who frees us from our addictions, from our self-made prisons. The Spirit breaks through all the barriers between people which cause human blight, so that class and race and sex are all transcended by the love of God through his Spirit. So the Spirit, far from being an anonymous power, becomes the living enrichment of Christ upon whose presence and encouragement the Christians depend for their lives.

In Jesus and Paul there is a profound reminder of the individual's relationship with God, but there is not a hint of what we now tend to call "individualistic" religion. Religion must have its springs in the individual heart, but these springs are part of a great river of the life of God, each person being a member of the Body, a branch of the Vine. The Spirit is given in the fellowship of the Church.

So for the Christian, verse 11 of Psalm 51 is filled up with the desire to be one with Christ, and not to be in that deathly place where we cut ourselves off from His love and turn our hearts away from His presence. No wonder Christians were afraid that they might so sin against the Holy Spirit that the profound gifts of God would be lost for ever. But the picture of the Prodigal Son encourages us to return in trust and penitence to our Father for the thousandth time. It was the terrible punishment of Cain that he was driven out to be a fugitive and a wanderer, alienated from the earth and its strength. His envy and murder of his brother closed his heart to God's presence. How many times in our lives, through our unredeemed feelings, thoughts and actions do we make ourselves an outsider, a fugitive, a wanderer without the Spirit of God to hold us in our integrity and dwell in our soul? St Augustine spoke from his own experience: "By my doing . . . the uprightness of my spirit hath been made old and bowed . . . when a man doth make himself stoop unto earthly lusts, he is 'bowed' in a manner, but when he is made erect for things above, upright is his heart made, in order that God may be good to him."[11]

Whilst it is often the case that we, as individuals or as the Church, turn our backs upon God, He remains in a dynamic and living relationship with us. We feel the absence of God, we long for His love, we thirst for His Spirit. Yet there is a sort of spiritless religion which owes more to habit and formal function than to this living relationship. The institutional Church, trapped as it often is, sometimes demonstrates to its members and to outsiders this spiritless existence. It is as though the systems are like the thistles or the rocky soil which inhibit the growth of the harvest. This prayer of the psalmist for a new and right spirit should not be just the prayer of the individual Christian, but the prayer of the Church. "Yet," as St Paul said, "always there is hope" (1 CORINTHIANS 13). Although we do experience such spiritless Christianity, we can also be inspired and cheered by the abundance of God's life in the Church, like the new shoots growing from a fallen tree. We demonstrate all the signs of anxiety and splitting which being cast away from God's presence bring, yet always we are within a heartbeat of being open to God and being fashioned by Him for His purpose. We are no different in this from the churches to whom the Spirit spoke in the Book of Revelation, and the call to obedience and to grace remains the same. God has not withdrawn His offer of the Holy Spirit, and we live on in that reality and that hope.

Much of the secular world seems cut off from the presence and spirit of God. The fugitives and wanderers are not just the addicts and the pushers, the criminals and the worshippers of the Golden Calf, but also those who sit at home and do not belong to anyone because they have always been afraid of commitment, those who have put themselves in isolation for fear of the nasty world, those who snipe at others who have the courage to be and to do, those who must have a scapegoat for the emptiness they feel themselves. Jesus told this parable; there was a man who had an evil spirit. The evil spirit was driven out by the power of God and went wandering in the world and found many other and worse evil spirits who then returned together to the man, who was still empty. They happily took possession. When I, as an individual, and we, as a society, are empty, we provide space for all the life-damaging and destructive energies in the creation we inhabit. The best way to resist weeds in a garden is to fill it with healthy, beautiful plants. Just to weed it, only creates an empty space.

So we are all touched by spiritless life. Whether we know it through our drifting or our despair or that cold cover-up of our real selves, it is an experience which in our hearts we recognize, although we don't all use the same language to describe it. So it is that we can pray with the psalmist:

## Psalm 51

*O give me the gladness of your help again:*
*and support me with a willing spirit.*

The Revised Standard Version of the Bible translates this
as "Restore to me the joy of thy salvation". When we find
the Spirit or when the Spirit finds us, there is a sense of
coming back to ourselves, of coming home, even if we have
never been there before. There is a recognition of what we
have been searching for – what we have been hiding –
what we have been evading. It has been one of the great
privileges of being a bishop to be told, week in week out,
by people who have become Christians in their adult life,
of their discovery of a new life. They bubble over with the
hope of a change in themselves, with the experience of seeing
things in a different way, of finding ways through their most
difficult jammed relationships. Every time I say the
confirmation blessing, "Almighty and everliving God, you
have given your servants new birth in baptism by water
and the Spirit, and have forgiven them all their sins,"[12] I
look at the candidates and imagine what those words, if
they were received, would mean, and try to apply them to
myself. To be restored to my true self is to experience a
freedom which, once I have tasted it, is the most desirable
thing in life. Salvation is a big, beautiful, sadly neglected
word, describing the renewed man or woman, reborn to
the wholeness which God gives. "Support me with a willing
spirit" – over and over again this is the prayer which the
struggling disciple asks of God. We know that, however
hard we try – and try we must – there is a sense in which
the willing spirit ("motive power" as Weiser describes it)
comes as a gift from outside or beyond ourselves, to spring

up within us like the pure clear water from the hillside, through rock and peat and heather.

The "motive power" – or lack of it – is the key to so much of our living. In east London the Church has been trying, with others, to find ways of involving local young people in the training and job opportunities created by the London Docklands. The first battle was to persuade those who are in the whole development for profit that they had a responsibility for their physical and social environment. The methods of development, the use of land, the price of property, the cheek-by-jowl existence of the penthouses and decaying estates, the priority of bringing people in from outside to work – all these policies contributed to the feelings of hopelessness, and indeed gave excuses for youngsters to switch off their own responsiblity for themselves. They know that many of their mates have done a year's training leading nowhere, they know that others can survive by doing unofficial jobs on the side, and their motivation to train is extinguished. So we are faced with a willingness to provide the training opportunities, but a lack of motivation. I have seen so many examples of this death of motivation, sometimes as a result of propaganda, sometimes as the result of long and depressing experience of defeat at the hands of an unjust and uncaring society – but, through whatever cause, the "willing spirit" has died or been diverted to absorbing and destructive patterns, or that terrible apathy and lethargy which creep round a soul which has no perceived purpose.

The language of God suggests to every human being that he or she is of value and has the dignity of being made to be like God. As our image of ourselves is battered and reduced by people's view of us, by the rejection and humiliation we experience, it is only too easy for us to lose sight — if we ever glimpsed it — of being a loved, affirmed and treasured child of God. So many people have lost the ability to see themselves as possessing a destiny, a purpose. This must be one of the great lessons of the growth of the Church in Latin America, where the poor and suffering people have found in their study of the Bible an affirmation of their own purpose in life, and have begun to walk tall in slums and afflicted villages. When this Spirit of God bubbles up within us, the stagnant rubbish is cleared away, and though it only begins as a spring, it soon gathers pace and generates power. Somehow we have to discover the way of unlocking the motivation, the willing spirit, through the truth of God. We should not think for a moment that we can do this without identifying with the battle against the social injustice, the corporate idolatry, the gluttony which squeezed and reduced the image that the people had of themselves. Salvation is not just something for the individual, though it is the most important fact of life for any individual — it is also about the wholeness and harmony of the kingdom of God, which we pray day by day will come on earth as in heaven.

\* \* \* \* \*

*Then will I teach transgressors your ways:*
*and sinners shall turn to you again.*

To experience the Spirit of God, to discover what it is like to be restored, to share in the "liberty and splendour of the children of God", is to become an enthusiast. At first

sight this looks like the psalmist trying to bribe God —
"If you save me, I'll convert everyone to you" — but it is
not like that. The psalmist already knows what being in love
with God is like. He has already glimpsed the joy, the
renewal and the cleansing and he knows that if he comes
back into harmony with God he won't be able to keep quiet
about it. Just as the person who has recently fallen in love
overflows with that love, not always sensitive to the state
and condition of others, so enthusiasm can sometimes claim
knowledge we do not possess, experience we never had,
solutions which do not exist, and worse — righteousness
which is not visible to anyone else. The Church is suspicious
of enthusiasm which flares up for a moment but then dies
away because there is no deep, well-built base to the fire.
Yet I also want to say that we, as a Church are far too timid
about our faith. In a world of aggressive ideologies, of
rampant all-conquering materialism, of massive injustice,
of considerable personal spiritual void, Christians are often
as quiet as mice, just making the occasional squeak. We
are so afraid of the scandals of aggressive, dictatorial, self-
righteous religion that we tend to reverse into hardly daring
to mention God and remaining shy about our allegiance
to Christ. I am sure this is one reason why we have relatively
few men in our churches in east London, because the spirit
of the age, expressed in the macho male, crushes the
tenderness, gentleness, strength and courage which flow from
loving depedence upon God. It is quite an act of faith in
our world to admit that we go to church — and yet the
Christ we follow is the Christ of all our lives, and in almost
all our struggles he is there before us. The most effective
way of converting people is by being the people God wants

us to be, but we should not be afraid to speak about our renewed life.

* * * * *

*O Lord God of my salvation, deliver me from bloodshed: and my tongue shall sing of your righteousness.*

This verse is difficult to understand because of the problems caused by the Hebrew word translated as "bloodshed" or "blood guiltiness". It could mean "save me from death" caused by sickness or violence. It could also mean "save me from the guilt associated with some violent bloodshed I have committed in the past or might commit in the future." Weiser suggests that it refers to the possibility that the psalmist would lose his life through no fault of his own, by a sort of guilt of association. The word in its simplest interpretation means literally "bloods".

It is not easy for us to clamber back into the way of thinking of the author of the psalm. He lived in a time when the rules of the book of Leviticus were untouched by the radical teaching of Christ, when, as I have already mentioned, cripples, menstruating women, lepers, deformed limbs, were viewed as unclean and in some sense an offence to God's holiness. Then Jesus touched the untouchable and taught that it is not what goes into a man when he eats which defiles him, but what comes out of his heart and mind. Blood guiltiness conjures up that world of sacrifices, of ritual cleansing, which seems so foreign to our way of thinking. Yet blood and life cannot be separated. I wonder what the haemophiliac feels about the blood he or she has received which has transferred the AIDS virus. Perhaps "deliver me from bloods" or "blood guiltiness" will take on a new and sombre meaning. To transfer to another person the results of our own behaviour must be an horrendous guilt to live with.

But while that is the most personal, direct and contemporary way of hidden "blood guiltiness", there are other ways in which we all are involved in the death and bloodshed of others. We cannot escape some responsibility for the deaths in wars caused by our own nation's activities, we cannot escape from some responsibility for death by starvation because of our nation's economic policies, we cannot escape some responsibility for the torture and oppression carried out by regimes to which our nation gives open or covert support. We all have a certain "blood guiltiness" before God. We are all part of the crowd crying, "Crucify him!" We are all part of the power which tried Him falsely, we are all tainted with the desire to punish someone which brought Him to trial. So this prayer to be delivered from blood guiltiness, which at first sight looks archaic and primitive, leads us to the longing for the healing and purging of God, the liberation from our guilt through our own actions or by our corporate association. As we stand against the forces which bring poverty and affliction to our neighbour near at hand and our universal neighbour who is far off, we begin to experience the deliverance of Christ, who refused to be part of the cycle of violence, however justified it might have been. "Sheathe your sword" was His word of peace (JOHN 18:11). Yet we have to live out our life in this world. Nations engage in the violence of power and economic strength, and then condemn the violence eventually resorted to by those who have tried for years to resist that power and slavery by peaceful means. It seems to be inevitable that we are caught up in blood guiltiness. As Oliver Tambo, the leader of the African National Congress, said after years of withholding from violence in South Africa, "When did the United Kingdom, indeed when did the Church of England, become pacifist?" In reality we have to strive as best we can to work for justice and for peace, but recognize in the sadness and evil of our world that when we come to our Maker we shall all have blood guiltiness on our hands.

\*   \*   \*   \*   \*

*O Lord open my lips:*
*and my mouth shall proclaim your praise.*

These are some of the most familiar words of the Old Testament, because of their centuries of use in the worship of the Church, but also therefore especially in danger of neglect precisely because of their familiarity. The psalmist has just prayed that his tongue may sing of his deliverance, and yet it is almost as though he cannot open his mouth because of what he fears about himself. He asks God even to open his lips, because he is so aware of his need for forgiveness, of his having forfeited the right to praise God through his uncleanness and the uncleanness of his lips. There are so many people who do not come to church because they do not feel good enough. They feel that to worship in church would be an act of hypocrisy. This way of thinking is a fundamental mistake, because those of us who do go to church and worship God go because we are not good enough to stay away or to manage on our own.

Jesus' story of the man who was justified before God in the synagogue described him as a man who stood at the back and didn't know what to say, and certainly had nothing to claim. The man who stood at the front and thanked God for his own goodness left the synagogue just as lost as when he went in.

We don't know how to pray, and it is true that the world's greatest acknowledged experts would say that they have only reached the foot of the mountain of prayer. I have sometimes discovered in the Church a sort of tight-lipped worship built more upon fear than on love. It is so nervous that the rules are going to be broken, that something real might emerge, that people might laugh or cry, that the lips grow tight. If we are tight-lipped in our worship, firmly repressing our hearts and minds, we shall be tight-lipped in our lives, preventing ourselves from sharing the warmth and spontaneity and love that abound in this world. So when I say "O Lord open my lips", I mean "open myself", "open other people here", to believe in your generosity, to believe in the wonder of faith, to encourage us to give ourselves into the love of God. I admire Peter's reaction to Jesus, when Jesus wanted to wash his feet (John 13). Peter was horrified – "You, Lord, wash my feet?" Jesus pointed out that Peter was cutting himself off from the love and generosity of God, behind his own view of things. But Peter immediately begged that Jesus wash not only his feet but wash him all over. That is how I see this verse. It is not only a plea to God to give us the right words and the right worship, but also a plea that God, in our worship, will help us to be open to Him in any way He chooses. It is a body, mind and soul, whole life experience, an expression of love and being loved that should wash us all over – open our lips, our arms, our whole selves to receive the healing power of God, through singing and reflecting and meditating and loving and eating and drinking and kneeling and standing and breathing and longing and hoping and trusting. When all that is released, we experience praise to God our Father, who made us, and God the Son, who saved us, and God the Spirit, who is even now making us a temple for Himself.

Sometimes when I am walking the dog in Mile End as the sun comes up, and I see the grey clouds suddenly touched with rose and apricot, and the heron stands on the path, grey like the clouds, backed by red double-decker buses, and even the Mile End Road is touched with beauty, I want to sing *Benedicite* (and do sometimes – let the reader beware!). It is always an experience of being opened up by God to see the beauty that hovers behind the ugliness, the love which shines through the grime, and it is above all the gift of God. All I needed to do was to be there and waiting.

* * * * *

*You take no pleasure in sacrifice or I would give it:*
*burnt offerings you do not want.*
*The sacrifice of God is a broken spirit:*
*a broken and contrite heart O God you will not despise.*

Criticism of the sacrificial system formed a strong and radical part of the prophets' teaching. These verses, too, represent a bold challenge to the vested interests of the worship of the Temple, and condemn the escape from personal religion into the functional, arms-length satisfaction of a religious system. There is a sense in which an "objective sacrifice" would bring comfort, because it is something we can do to ward off the feeling of guilt, or something we can offer when we receive so much.

But the secular tide has swept us away from the world of the psalmist, where God or gods were all around – under every tree, behind every door, in every act of life. Being right with God was central to life at that time, and there were both costly and cheap ways of getting there. The psalmist describes the cheap way of making sacrifices. This way was not cheap originally, but only by habit. Ask a farmer whether he is willing to give a cow for his sins, or a business man his shares. The sacrifice began as something costly, but became something cheap. The psalmist, like the prophets, returns to the true sacrifice, the cost that counts, and when we look at it, we see that it is a fundamental question about the centre of our lives. This sacrifice which is pleasing to God is no once-a-week visit to church, nor a hobby like an interest in stamps or a football team, it is a sacrifice which begins at the centre of our selves. One of the reasons why I find it difficult to take too seriously the anger and arguments people express about exactly which words we ought to use in our worship of God, is the sense that such concentration upon our favourite words is like straining at a gnat and swallowing a camel. The whole encounter with God, the struggle with Him, the loving of Him, is so much more dynamic and life-changing than can be captured in a form of words. The central issue is not whether we address God in words from the first century, the sixteenth, the seventeenth or the twentieth, but rather what it means in our lives to address God at all. "The sacrifice of a broken spirit, a broken and contrite heart" — now that is fundamental. That derives from where we finally allow God into our citadel, where our defences are down, where we realize our dependence on God rather than hiding in our comic fortress, our sandcastle which cannot withstand the first touch from the first ripple from the first wave at the edge of the Ocean which is God.

We rush headlong, jostled along by our own desires, our own prejudices, our own treasured ideas and feelings, building our house on the sand, and then some storm or trauma or vision stops us, blows down the house we have built, and we are naked again. It is hard to see that God accepts that nakedness, and that brokenness. It is hard because our life prepares us always to build our own castle, to defend our own, to pursue our own, to gain our own. Yet strangely it is where our castle breaks that we find the breakthrough. It is when we realize that we are like the Prodigal Son, when we take into ourselves the recognition of how far we have gone from our peace, that we come close to our Father who is always waiting for us. It is no wonder that people have turned aside from this God who comes to us through our brokenness and contrition, because we have been persuaded to believe that happiness and well-being are of our own making, that our safety lies in self-defence, and that security lies in self-aggrandizement. But, says Jesus, "What will a man gain by winning the whole world, at the cost of his true self?" (MATTHEW 16:26). It is a hard lesson to take on board, and we resist it with all our pent-up self-reliance, but the wonder to be found through being vulnerable, through being broken, is what makes the heavens rejoice over one sinner who sees he is in the wrong. The broken and contrite heart is not despised, but received by God with eternal love.

\* \* \* \* \*

*In your graciousness do good to Zion:*
*rebuild the walls of Jerusalem.*
*Then will you delight in right sacrifices*
*in burnt-offerings and oblations:*
*then will they offer young bulls upon your altar.*

There seems to be no conceivable way that this can have been part of the original psalm. As a vicar who added contemporary verses to ancient hymns, I can quite understand that some time between the fall of Jerusalem in 586 BC and the rebuilding of the Temple in 444 BC, a priest felt that a balance needed to be struck. If the restoration of the Temple was to happen, there would have to be sacrificial giving as well as sacrificial living. He was probably right as well, because sometimes the surest sign that we have a broken and contrite heart is our willingness to get on with the practical generosity to which God has been calling us all along.

So ends the psalm as we have it. To read it over and over again teaches us to remember how it is between us and God. If you feel down-hearted after this study, then I have failed, because there is healing and hope at its heart. Yet I have to admit that the psalm has often left me with a sense of inadequacy and shame. For this reason I take its healing medicine with Psalm 103:10–16, which restore my sense of the merciful love of God.

He has not dealt with us according to our sins:
nor rewarded us according to our wickedness.
For as the heavens are high above the earth:
so great is his mercy over those that fear him;
as far as the east is from the west:
so far has he set our sins from us.
As a father is tender towards his children:
so is the Lord tender to those that fear him.
For he knows of what we are made:
he remembers that we are but dust.
The days of man are but as grass:
he flourishes like a flower of the field;
when the wind goes over it, it is gone:
and its place will know it no more.

Here is the wonder of God's forgiveness as lived out in
Christ, restoring our dignity and value, encouraging a proper
sense of self-worth. We worship a God who does not make
the punishment fit the crime, who knows what we are made
of, because He brought us into being. He knows every low,
mean, bestial, obscene trick we can do. He sees the torture,
the cruelty and the dishonesty that lie in man. He
contemplates the staining and damage we do to His own
image in us. Yet looking all that in the face, His verdict,
proposed in Psalm 103, is like that of His Son on the cross:
"Father, forgive them."

This forgiveness is not a soft option. God did not say
that our failures and our wickedness are not important. No,
He recognizes the seriousness of what we do, yet, as a father,
has compassion on His children. We know how to forgive
our children because our love for them overwhelms us, just

as His love for us moves beyond the severity to the love and compassion. When people try to persuade me to believe in the subhuman God who would create men, women and children for eternal torment, I return to these words and to the face of Christ for the truth.

Being a bishop has made me even more aware of just how high and deep and broad the love and forgiveness of God has to be. I experience a desperate falling short of my own expectations of myself, of others' expectations of me, let alone of what God expects of me. Perhaps when God reflects upon the whole sinfulness of the human race my sins will not rate much, but to me they still seem great and unforgivable. Yet always there is God, with His forgiveness as high as the sky, and His arms outstretched to hold us, as wide as East is from West. In one sense I thank God that I am not righteous (I hope that doesn't sound wrong), because if I was righteous I believe my relationships with people would be *"de haut en bas"*. As it is, we are all in the same mess together – bishop, alcoholic, penitent thief – and the promise to us all is the same, that we can be with Him in paradise. It is not just my own sins, but the sins of the world, in which I share. We are all caught up in the world's shame, compromised, timid and stained. Yet in these great and gracious words we are called to look up to the wonder of God and bathe in His love which shines like the sun. So we share in that primeval experience of which Charles Wesley helped us sing:

> 'Tis mercy all, immense and free;
> for, O my God, it found out me.

# PSALM 90
## God Yesterday,
## Today and Forever

*Lord you have been our refuge:*
*from one generation to another.*

*Before the mountains were born*
*or the earth and the world were brought to be:*
*from eternity to eternity you are God.*

*You turn man back into dust:*
*saying, "Return to dust you sons of Adam."*

*For a thousand years in your sight*
*are like yesterday passing:*
*or like one watch of the night.*

*You cut them short like a dream:*
*like the fresh grass of the morning;*

*in the morning it is green and flourishes:*
*at evening it is withered and dried up.*

*And we are consumed by your anger:*
*because of your indignation we cease to be.*

*You have brought our iniquities before you:*
*and our secret sins to the light of your countenance.*

*Our days decline beneath your wrath:*
*and our years pass away like a sigh.*

*The days of our life are three score years and ten*
*or if we have strength four score:*
*the pride of our labours is but toil and sorrow*
*for it passes quickly away and we are gone.*

*Who can know the power of your wrath:*
*who can know your indignation like those that fear you?*

*Teach us so to number our days:*
*that we may apply our hearts to wisdom.*

*Relent, O Lord, how long will you be angry?*
*take pity on your servants.*

*O satisfy us early with your mercy:*
*that all our days we may rejoice and sing.*

*Give us joy for all the days you have afflicted us:*
*for the years we have suffered adversity.*

*Show your servants your work:*
*and let their children see your glory.*

*May the glorious favour of the Lord our God*
   *be upon us:*
*prosper the work of our hands*
*O prosper the work of our hands!*

In my mind this psalm is set in the Battle of Britain. I was only three at the time, so the picture must have been created by the cinema and the history books. I see congregations gathered in village churches, with Spitfires flying overhead tracing the battle for our nation in the skies. The congregation is singing:

> O God, our help in ages past,
> Our hope for years to come,
> Our shelter from the stormy blast
> And our eternal home.

The same psalm was being sung no doubt in Lutheran churches in Germany, and amongst secret gatherings of Jews it will have been recited as the Holocaust gathered its horrific momentum.

It sets us human beings in the perspective of the eternal God, recognizing His power and His wrath, yet asking for mercy and goodness for the future following the years of affliction. The psalm was so precious to the people of Israel that it alone in the psalter was ascribed to Moses, yet it is also a song of universal significance and application. Here we wrestle with our transient nature before eternal God and express the universal longing for peace and satisfaction on earth. Perhaps it is a psalm we need to free of its nationalistic usage and find a broader message for the sons of Adam.

\* \* \* \* \*

> *Lord you have been our refuge*
> *From one generation to another.*

One of the fascinating appeals of Judaism is that devout Jews find their main identity from their faith and from their community of faith rather than from their nation. To share in *Seder* is to be joined with Jews throughout the world celebrating in their families the Passover of God. It is not the same as having a dual nationality but rather having a higher allegiance to their Lord who is the Lord of all creation.

Perhaps it is in Israel itself that this significant fact is most likely to be forgotten, because there nationality takes over from community of faith. It is certainly this latter understanding which gives a special tone to the words "Lord you have been our refuge from one generation to another."

The worshipper looks back through the genealogy of their own specific family and at the same time recognizes the continuity of the people of God from the promise made to Abraham down to the present day. They are addressing God who has helped them survive as a people every conceivable terror and suffering. As each symbol in the Passover meal is shared — the unleavened bread of affliction, the bitter herbs of slavery, the Passover lamb of their freedom — they are joined together from generation to generation in a community of faith and family. For English Christians the hymn has expressed the faith that God cares for our nation. Perhaps there was a time when we felt that we could be identified as a Christian country, that our patriotism and our faith in Christ seemed natural together — but the Scots and the Welsh and the Irish have often had their doubts! As Christianity has become a minority faith in this country, it has become more difficult to see ourselves as a Christian nation, though the framework remains. Many Christians do not now see "my Country — right or wrong" as expressing their allegiance to our Lord. It was fascinating and encouraging to rediscover at the Lambeth Conference of 1988 a worldwide Christian identity and history which expressed our Christian allegiance more deeply and broadly than any narrow nationalism. In our Bible studies and our worship and our deliberations we were responding to a community of faith, not just to a national heritage.

Many of us do not come from generations of Christian people, we do not have the tradition of family prayer and family worship, nor have we ever known as a family what it would mean to have a Christian identity apart from a broad cultural meaning. So this opening verse refers for Christians to the continuum of the Christian church throughout the world, of which we have become members by baptism and the laying on of hands. Our "family" meal is the Eucharist, our bearers of tradition are the Bible and the common prayers, and our focus of identity is Christ. We hope and pray that God will protect our nation, that He will continue to call us to great responsibilities in the worldwide community, that His Kingdom may continue to influence the structure, laws and culture of our kingdom. But we serve two kingdoms whom we pray may be one, but always recognizing that our higher allegiance is to the Kingdom of God. So the "our" in this psalm refers to the people of God throughout all ages, including the Jewish community, sons and daughters of Abraham, from whom we sprang through Jesus Christ son of David. Our localized human ancestry is precious and valued, and God has loved us in the context of our rather British way, but the stream of consciousness which comes from a more direct and overt relationship with God is a stream tied not to nationality but to faith.

\* \* \* \* \*

*Before the mountains were born*
*or the earth and the world were brought to be:*
*from eternity to eternity you are God.*

"I am Alpha and Omega, the beginning and the end." These are the words spoken by Him who sits on the throne to John in the Book of Revelation. "When all things began, the Word already was. The Word dwelt with God, and what God was, the Word was. The Word, then, was with God at the beginning, and through him all things came to be" (JOHN 1:1–2). With these visions the Christian revelation follows through the implications of the incarnation. If Jesus Christ was God made man, then Christ was pre-existent with God from eternity to eternity. Expressions like "before time began" carry logical difficulties! For something to be "before" something else, there must have been continuity of existence which implies time, which makes "before time began" a non-sense. But this problem is caused by our own difficulty in crossing between the eternal and temporal dimensions. We only have the dimensions we can measure and recognize, to describe or use as parables of the dimensions we do not see. So heaven becomes a beautiful place with meadows and rivers and perfect cities. So eternity becomes everlasting, that is life freed from the limitations of time. So the Kingdom of God derives from His throne in Heaven, and His "court" becomes the heavenly beings – the angels and archangels more or less in supernatural appearance. But the cherubim and seraphim, paradise, the inferno, the company of all the saints in everlasting peace, are all parables of God's dimension invisible to us and "hid from our eyes". Plato pointed to the greater reality of eternity by suggesting that the earth and we players in the drama are only shadows on a wall. It is hard for us down-to-earth, pragmatic, twentieth-century, secular people to envisage a society for whom heaven was more real than earth. The idea seems weird. I have already talked about the "City of God" (Psalm 46) which is another spatial parable of the place where God dwells. Perhaps all we can ever do is tell parables and then realize how inadequate they are. But we need not only to open our imagination and lift the turret of our mind to look at the sky, but also to explore new parables, lasers, computers, x-rays, radio astronomy, genetic engineering, nuclear physics; all may be the bearers of new analogies to Eternal God's way of giving birth and sustenance to the universe. We need to find a credible, thinkable parable to express the wonder of faith which was able to say "The Word, then, was with God at the beginning, and through Him all things came to be." The pre-existence of God, whether in oneness or in Trinity, challenges us to draw analogies from our studies of the universe.

"For all that may be known of God by men lies plain before their eyes . . . His invisible attributes, that is to say his everlasting power and deity, have been visible, ever since the world began, to the eye of reason, in the things he has made" (ROMANS 1:19-20). Yet it is primarily in prayer that the vision of God in eternity is grasped, because prayer itself is a bridging activity. When we pray we put ourselves into the realm of the Spirit of God. We attempt to cross into the foothills of eternity and sense the mountain towering, secure and ineffable, above us as we pause to ponder the majesty of it all. So in our transient, temporal moment we address and relate to the "Thou" through whom the universe is made. Weiser's translation helps: "Before the mountains were brought forth and the earth and the world were formed in travail, thou art God", from eternity to eternity.

\* \* \* \* \*

> *You turn man back into dust:*
> *saying, "Return to dust you sons of Adam."*

The contemplation of God only serves to sharpen our sense of impermanence. We are threatened with being nameless and without a destiny. Anyone who has scattered the ashes of someone they loved feels this fragile, vulnerable identity crisis. "Return to dust, you sons of Adam." Can this mortal flesh inherit eternity, or are intimations of immortality a fantasy to comfort us in our short and withering time on earth?

> *You cut them short like a dream:*
> *like the fresh grass of the morning;*
> *in the morning it is green and flourishes:*
> *at evening it is withered and dried up.*
> . . .
> *The days of our life are three score years and ten*
> *or if we have strength four score:*
> *the pride of our labours is but toil and sorrow*
> *for it passes quickly away and we are gone.*

We are children of the natural world, like grass and flowers and animals. Our stay is brief, like a dream which for a moment seems so vivid and real, yet which dies away when we wake. Human beings cling to life with amazing passion even when it contains almost nothing recognizable as life. "The days of our life are three score years and ten, or if we have strength four score: the pride of our labours is but toil and sorrow, for it passes quickly away and we are gone." Here again is the pessimism of the Preacher in Ecclesiastes. After contemplating all his achievements, all his pleasures, he recognizes their transience. "Alas, wise man and fool die the same death! So I came to hate life, since everything that was done here under the sun was a trouble to me; for all is emptiness and chasing the wind" (ECCLESIASTES 2:17-18). But here the despairing look at the impermanence of man is only a prelude to the affirmation of the reality of God. In the Old Testament the vision for the human being is of a righteous, prosperous and happy life based upon trust in God, but in the New Testament the hope is in the resurrection to new life with God in eternity. Our Jewish heritage prevents us from pious otherworldliness and makes us get on with our earthly life in faith, and our Christian revelation points us beyond the three score years and ten to the wonder of the heavenly life with God which puts this earthly struggle in perspective. "For I reckon that the sufferings we now endure bear no comparison with the splendour, as yet unrevealed, which is in store for us . . . yet always there was hope, because the universe itself is to be freed from the shackles of mortality and enter upon the liberty and splendour of the children of God" (ROMANS 8:18, 20, 21).

So we are to see our transient lives as a preparation for glory. Although they are limited to four score years if we have the strength, they are nevertheless of eternal value and significance. It is clear to me that the people who cope best with the often painful years between three score years and ten and four score or more are those who see these years as a transition from physical life to life with God in eternity. There needs to be a letting go of dependence on our human achievement, an opening of the heart and mind to the space and scope of eternal God. The rose buds, blooms, fades and falls to the ground, bearing the seed of new life.

Part of the trouble is our pathetic lack of ritual, proper grieving and celebration at death. I love the picture in Manchester City gallery of the Viking warrior being launched out to sea to enter Valhalla, the Hall of the Slain, by fire and water. He lies there in glory as his ship is fired and he finds his eternal destiny. I grieve that our society has reduced our departure rites to a fifteen-minute timetable with the discreet casket slipping behind the crematorium curtain. It is no wonder we have so little sense of our eternal destination.

\* \* \* \* \*

> *For a thousand years in your sight*
> *are like yesterday passing:*
> *or like one watch of the night.*

People have described our accelerated culture as "instant", "three-minute", "disposable". We show signs of irresistible impatience. We have to give our answers in one minute, our "flexible friends" are there to take the waiting out of wanting, and the tape speeds up. Yet the psalmist here suggests that in God's time each generation is just an hour's watch, and every thousand years just like a day. We have had nearly two days since Christ on that reckoning. History is foreshortened under the prospect of eternity. To us, two years of frustration seem like a lifetime, three years unbearable. We plan to get everything done in months and years, and have almost no sense of decades and centuries. As we approach the end of the second millenium of Christ we shall ask ourselves great questions on the larger scale. The theologian and the historian know how many times the same issues, the same questions, the same answers recur in our history. That is what we would expect if in God's reality we are only two days from Christ. As Kierkegaard said, Christ is our contemporary. The issues raised by the psalms were present in the days of Solomon, alive and kicking in the days of Christ on earth, still troubling Augustine, causing Luther to change the Christian world, and now they confront us at the end of the second millenium. Each generation works at its own agenda but, if it has sense, always in the light of the past. We should examine the absurdity of our impatience in terms of the earth and in terms of our own destiny. Yet there is also an urgency because every time and every age can be God-bearing and every day we should be open to the advancement of God's kingdom. Jesus called us to be alert, awake, ready for his coming. He is the image of the invisible God – the same yesterday, today and forever.

\* \* \* \* \*

*We are consumed by your anger:*
*because of your indignation we cease to be.*
*You have brought our iniquites before you:*
*and our secret sins to the light of your countenance.*
*Our days decline beneath your wrath:*
*and our years pass away like a sigh.*

. . .

*Who can know the power of your wrath:*
*who can know your indignation like those that fear you?*

Our dying is related to our sin and is the result of the wrath of God. This is the way the psalmist viewed mortality. St

Paul declared that Adam died because of his disobedience, and we all died with him. "It was through one man that sin entered the world, and through sin death, and thus death pervaded the whole human race, inasmuch as all men have sinned." He tells this story because he has a wonderful solution: "God's act of grace is out of all proportion to Adam's wrongdoing. For if the wrongdoing of that one man brought death upon so many, its effect is vastly exceeded by the grace of God and the gift that came to so many by the grace of one man, Jesus Christ" (ROMANS 5:12–15). The wages of sin is death, but "As in Adam all men die, so in Christ all will be brought to life" (1 CORINTHIANS 15:22).

The psalms interpreted the three score years and ten or four score as the mortal span of the sons and daughters of Adam because of their sin. I don't think we believe this causation. We see ourselves as part of nature which brings its own limits, and through the gift of God there is a time to be born and a time to die. The sun shines and the rain pours on the just and the unjust. We are transient creatures. But the truth of the saying comes from the deaths which accompany our disobedience. The death of hope, the death of self-respect, the death of harmony, and perhaps finally within our hearts the death of God.

I have written elsewhere about the wrath of God. In Christ I am unable to see that wrath as separate from His love. I ask myself if this robs the wrath of its sanction and power to change me. But my encounters with God have persuaded me in Christ that it is all for love, and therefore in the last analysis His anger is "for us" – *pro nobis*. If love casts out fear, then in the end what place will there be for the terror that God's being could instil in us if He were to exercise

His power and righteousness? Such negative wrath would be contrary to His chief characteristic, which is love. Yet anger has its place in parenthood and anger is both a teacher and a resource in the formation of a child. So the anger of God against me, if it were not for Christ and the Advocate, would destroy any staying power I might have in my discipleship (see Psalm 51).

I find Weiser's translation of verse 11 helpful: "But who considers the power of thy anger, and who is afraid of thy wrath?"[1] I have known too many people who have been distorted and repressed by their fear of the anger of God. Yet at the same time I see in myself and indeed in a pale Christendom a forgetfulness of the anger of God, as though our world and ourselves were suddenly behaving as God would wish and wished from the beginning. So injustice and wickedness abound, we mutilate the world God has given us, we torture and imprison unjustly, we steal and live adulterous lives, we rob the poor and we waste the resources of the earth, yet we have no fear of God who gave us life. Perhaps we hide from the fear because we don't know the love, and it is only as we are bathed in the love that we have the courage to face the anger. So the psalmist prays:

> *Teach us so to number our days:*
> *that we may apply our hearts to wisdom.*

We are only given one life, whether it is four score years or less. We should recognize the scope of our life and value each day to learn and grow towards God. To learn wisdom in the psalmist's eyes, as in the eyes of the writer of the book of Proverbs, it is necessary to begin with humility before God, recognizing that we are a passing shadow. If we are open to God then we can be open-eyed to the universe. We are fitted with the right lens. Reverence is the key to wisdom and reverence has within it a proper fear of the awesome possibilities of our own freedom. We have the freedom to deny God and deaden Him within us. Our science seen as the glory of man may profoundly mislead us, our science done to the glory of God may lead us to truth. Our recognition of God and our role *vis-à-vis* God is essential to the search for wisdom. It may be natural to be clever and intelligent, it is God-given to be wise.

There are those who say that the psalm should be divided here, but I find the conclusion consistent with what has gone before — or if not totally consistent, at least expressive of faith as we live it.

*Relent, O Lord, how long will you be angry?*
*take pity on your servants.*
*O satisfy us early with your mercy:*
*that all our days we may rejoice and sing.*
*Give us joy for all the days you have afflicted us:*
*For the years we have suffered adversity.*
*Show your servants your work:*
*and let their children see your glory.*
*May the glorious favour of the Lord our God be upon us:*
*prosper the work of our hands*
*O prosper the work of our hands!*

This plea derives from what has gone before. Before eternal God we are just a blade of grass; we are trapped by our own sins and so we experience death. But we have seen the Lord and tasted his peace and we crave restoration. The writer has brought us to our knees in dependence on God, and for a moment our arrogance is quietened and we are ready at God's disposal, but the disease goes on. The years of affliction and adversity continue as we long for paradise on earth. We cry out to God that we may leave the shadow of death and enter into the sunlight of his mercy. We know that we need His mercy and His gift of the Spirit bringing repentance, but we are left with our freedom. We want to exercise our freedom in loving God, but we do not. There is a deep flaw and we continue to choose the wrong we do not want. We are fascinated by what leads to death, seduced by the deceiver who argues in our minds so skilfully to lead us away from life. So we pray, "Relent, O Lord – how long will you be angry – have pity on us and enable us by your love to choose freely the life you give." "Satisfy us . . ." "Give us joy . . ." "Show us your work and let our children see your glory . . ." "Prosper the work of our hands . . ." "Give us your gracious favour".

We long to live at peace with God, but we continue to live in the daily struggle of faith, finishing each day with its damage and healing done to us. This is our journey through life, and we pray that God in His mercy – our refuge from one generation to another – will bring us to eternal life. When we experience harmony with God, it brings divine consolation, and our hearts can sing silently of the glorious favour of our God.

# PSALM 104
## Creator of Heaven and Earth

*Bless the Lord O my soul:*
*O Lord my God how great you are!*

*Clothed with majesty and honour:*
*wrapped in light as in garment.*

*You have stretched out the heavens like a tent-cloth:*
*and laid the beams of your dwelling upon their waters;*

*you make the clouds your chariot:*
*and ride upon the wings of the wind;*

*you make the winds your messengers:*
*and flames of fire your ministers;*

*you have set the earth on its foundations:*
*so that it shall never be moved.*

*The deep covered it as with a mantle:*
*the waters stood above the hills.*

*At your rebuke they fled:*
*at the voice of your thunder they hurried away.*

*they went up to the mountains*
*they went down by the valleys:*
*to the place which you had appointed for them.*

## The Lord's Song

*You fixed a limit which they may not pass:*
*they shall not return again to cover the earth.*

*You send springs into the gullies:*
*which run between the hills;*

*they give drink to every beast of the field:*
*and the wild asses quench their thirst.*

*Beside them the birds of the air build their nests:*
*and sing among the branches.*

*You water the mountains from your dwelling on high:*
*and the earth is filled by the fruits of your work.*

*You cause the grass to grow for the cattle:*
*and all green things for the servants of mankind,*

*You bring food out of the earth:*
*and wine that makes glad the heart of man.*

*oil to give him a shining countenance:*
*and bread to strengthen his heart.*

*The trees of the Lord are well watered:*
*the cedars of Lebanon that he has planted,*

*where the birds build their nests:*
*and the stork makes her home in the pine-tops.*

*The high hills are a refuge for the wild goats:*
*and the crags a cover for the conies.*

*You created the moon to mark the seasons:*
*and the sun knows the hour of its setting.*

*You make darkness and it is night:*
*in which all the beasts of the forest move by stealth.*

*The lions roar for their prey:*
*seeking their food from God.*

*When the sun rises they retire:*
*and lay themselves down in their dens.*

*Man goes out to his work:*
*and to his labour until the evening.*

*Lord how various are your works:*
*in wisdom you have made them all*
*and the earth is full of your creatures.*

*There is the wide immeasurable sea:*
*there move living things without number*
*great and small:*

*there go the ships to and fro:*
*and there is that Leviathan*
*whom you formed to sport in the deep.*

*These all look to you:*
*to give them their food in due season.*

*When you give it to them they gather it:*
*when you open your hand they are satisfied with*
  *good things.*

*When you hide your face they are troubled:*
*when you take away your breath*
*they die and return to their dust.*

*When you send forth your spirit they are created:*
*and you renew the face of the earth.*

*May the glory of the Lord endure for ever:*
*may the Lord rejoice in his works.*

*If he look upon the earth it shall tremble:*
*if he but touch the mountains they shall smoke.*

*I will sing to the Lord as long as I live:*
*I will praise my God while I have any being.*

*May my meditation be pleasing to him:*
*for my joy shall be in the Lord.*

*May sinners perish from the earth*
*let the wicked be no more:*
*bless the Lord O my soul*
*O praise the Lord.*

"Bless the Lord, my soul." This great song to God begins with the fundamental human experience. These words are enough for a book in themselves, and then it would not have been said, because this concerns the whole yearning of human beings to love and praise their Maker. I do not know what it would be like to be an eagle – perhaps the eagle is not aware of what it is like to be an eagle – but somehow, as the eagle glides across a vast expanse of mountain and valley, there is praise. We have the added gift of self-consciousness, and we look at the creation around us – the butterfly which settles on our hand; the massive waves crashing on the rocks; the breathtaking brilliance of the human brain – and it stops us in our tracks. It is beyond us, it is given to us, we cannot help but look to the One who gave it all the energy to be. Our talent is to see the universe and wonder, and to feel an increased personal significance. My soul is not diminished by the Milky Way and the toucan — it is enriched and expanded. I may be small, infinitesimal, as I finally stand on the mountain peak, but my soul is soaring where the eagle flies.

It is difficult to see how I or anyone else can, by argument, persuade a person to see it like that. If he or she experiences the grandeur of the mountains in a way which does not call from a secret place the desire to bless the Lord God — then it is hard to explain. There must also be a source of blessing and hope for those who look upon the earth and the stars as an accident, but in the believer's encounter with nature, with life and splendour, there is a Godness, there is a "You" speaking in a still small voice to the "me" who looks and wonders. As we copy and extract the skills and resources of this beautiful earth, we can see the wonder in the man-made eagles and brains and organs, but in a sense they are only a reflection, a derivation from what is given.

We also see the horrendous sights which make us agonize and question the creator — the locusts attracted to the last crops of a dying tribe, the cancer riotously distorting the head of a much-loved friend, the grotesque sights of the mutual eating which is the way of the earth. Whatever else the camera has shown us, it has provided enough evidence to kill any romanticism about the world about us. My own unfavourite sight was of a large toad consuming a river crab like a fat face crunching whitebait. But although we cannot understand — although a part of us rebels against a creation built on mutual digestion, life, decay and regeneration —

nevertheless we cannot resist the wonder and majesty of it all. The person who I am, sees and reaches up to God and wants to love and adore the "You" who inbreathes it all. To me, it remains unthinkable, or at least unbelievable, that what I see is here through some age-long, headlong, continuous accident. To bless the Lord is a sort of healing process for the tired, drained and cynical side of my soul – as if a therapy were taking place, restoring wholeness and humility.

\*   \*   \*   \*   \*

*O Lord my God how great you are!*
*Clothed with majesty and honour:*
*wrapped in light as in a garment.*
*You have stretched out the heavens like a tent-cloth:*
*and laid the beams of your dwelling upon their waters;*
*you make the clouds your chariot:*
*and ride upon the wings of the wind;*
*you make the winds your messengers:*
*and flames of fire your ministers.*

The greatness of God's being. It is an easy mistake to worship the creation – perhaps we all do. We know what it is like to feel our legs weaken at the sight of a beautiful person, or to be caught up in a piece of music. It is not at all difficult for me to understand why the ancient people worshipped the sun and moon, the massive bull with its sexual power, the cornfields bearing food, the wine bringing a sense of well-being. I find it less easy to understand the worship of stereos and BMWs or computers, because to me they are so obviously man-made tools, and to worship such is a little comical or pathetic. But the psalmist was aware of the battle with the worship of other gods who were real and seemed to have good cash value. It was important, therefore, to state over and over again the Godness of God, and God's being as distinct from all the wondrous universe He had created. The poet attempted the impossible – to describe the Godhead beyond the whole creation – in God's own space, in God's own being.

He used the picture of the Lord "above the firmament" to establish God's "otherness" to what He had made. We have no idea what sort of space or time God occupies. We do not think of the earth as set on pillars, nor of the waters above the sky. It is one of the sad absurdities of the way we look at these great poems and other texts in the Bible that we try to see these visions as physical realities, rather than rest in their imagery to point us to God beyond the barriers of our perception. There should be less difficulty for us to grasp the possiblility of a hidden dimension, when so much has been revealed to us of realities around us which in earlier days people could not see.

When Elijah escaped to the holy mountain, God was not in the earthquake, nor in the great wind, nor the fire, but in the still small voice – the whisper from God's side of the veil which conceals and reveals God's very being. The psalmist's picture is of the Great God clothed in light, supreme above the skies which He rolled out like a tent to be His palace – where the rays of His beauty paint the amazing splendour of the sky in storm or still sunset. It is only a picture of something we know and see, being used to inspire in us the sense of that reality – the space of God whose Being we do not see. In all the current anxiety about the ozone layer, the idea of a "tent" set over us by God to protect the earth gains a new meaning. So great is our arrogance that we have even torn holes in that.

When Moses penetrated to the meeting place with God on Mount Horeb, he was told God's name – "I am, that is who I am." It is a mystery beyond our grasp, yet pointing to the faith that God not only is, but is the source of all being. He is in Himself (this is not a matter of gender) and He acts within and through all the creation, which depends for its life on Him.

\* \* \* \* \*

*When you hide your face they are troubled:*
*when you take away their breath*
*they die and return to their dust.*
*When you send forth your spirit they are created:*
*and you renew the face of the earth.*

His Being contains within Him all the potential of the universe, for there is no being without God. But God is not just God of being – as it were, existing in some wondrous eternal plateau. God is a God of action, a living God, a God who creates, sustains, renews the creation, and it is this act of creation to which the poet now turns.

In verses 5 – 9 the poet describes his own understanding of how the earth came to be. God fixed the earth firmly on its foundations so that it could not be shaken, and then covered the earth with the sea so that the waters lay over the mountains. Then God rebuked the sea and it ran down into the valleys to an appointed place, and God set boundaries for the water, to hold it in so that it would not run back and cover the earth. From where the psalmist sat, knowing what he knew, that seemed a fair description. We can see how the poet and his contemporaries may have thought that. Through the centuries, whole new insights have been gained into the way the universe and our earth came to be. The story we are now piecing together is still far short of complete knowledge – a possible vast explosion and the earth spinning off like a ball of volcanic fire and cooling down and taking shape through primeval collisions as land mass crunched into land mass and threw up the mountains, as the basic life forms gave way to more and more developed life forms, until the human being emerged, and the earth rotating round the sun as part of the solar system in one of many galaxies. In one sense, it makes no difference exactly how the creation came to be, it can be seen as the creative activity of a transcendent being. The Church has sometimes made itself look absurd by defending the story of the creation in seven days, by accepting the cosmology of ancient times without recognizing that the point is not *how* the creation came to be, but that God was and is the source of it. The key contrast is between those who say that the whole universe came to be by some fluke contrived by a billion years, and those who believe it is the creation of the living God. It is that difference which affects our sense of being human in this exquisite and alarming setting. The creation story in Genesis may tie in with the latest scientific description, or it may not; but that does not affirm or deny the great truth being claimed by the writers, that in the beginning there was God. It is the message of the Bible that God was the beginning – God is the sustaining life of creation, and God is its destiny. That is the religious truth expressed

through the amazed and wondering eyes of each generation.
The miracle of being has its source in God.

> *You have set the earth on its foundations:*
> *so that it shall never be moved.*
> *The deep covered it as with a mantle:*
> *the waters stood above the hills.*
> *At your rebuke they fled:*
> *at the voice of your thunder they hurried away;*
> *they went up to the mountains*
> *they went down by the valleys:*
> *to the place which you had appointed for them.*
> *You fixed a limit which they may not pass:*
> *they shall not return again to cover the earth.*

We have to find a way of imagining God in our day. The
twentieth-century mind has to tune in to the eternal creator.
The psalms are songs of God, they are the music of His
Word. But we also have to discover our own language and
hear our own heavenly music. There is a hill in Kent where
I go when east London gets too much for me. I stand on
that hill from time to time and watch the earth turn through
the day, the year pass through the seasons. Once, when I
was there in the autumn, I saw a flock of starlings – perhaps
as many as three thousand sitting on the telegraph wires.
They were chattering away to each other, then suddenly,
in a great rush of wings which left the telegraph wires
swinging, they swarmed overhead in a cloud. I wondered
what the person had said on the phone that had so shocked
them! It all seemed so miraculous – the wires carrying the
conversations, millions and millions of messages, by wire,
by satellite, all over the world, out to space and back. The

starlings, too, talked incessantly, bound together by a single voice saying, "This is the time to flock, this is the time to move."

I was amazed at the thought of all the voices of the earth and the skies on the airwaves — voices of people, of all creatures. On the same hill I see the swallows arrive from Africa in the spring, and in October see them set off thousands of miles on a route they know by the voice of instinct, which leads them to their winter home and guides them back to the same roof, the same eaves, in the priory where I stay.

I thought, too, of those great radio telescopes, picking up signals from the furthest galaxies we know. I think of the communication going on between the cells of my own body, the way in which, through the microchip of my own mind, I can travel back into the voices, feelings, pictures of my childhood in Gloucestershire. There is sound, conversation, laughter, signals, cries of terror, pain, filling the consciousness of the universe.

This idea was overwhelming to me when I first thought it, but I found it had been thought before by the psalmist.

> The heavens tell out the glory of God,
>     the vault of heaven reveals his handiwork.
> One day speaks to another,
> night with night shares its knowledge,
>       and this without speech or language
>       or sound of any voice.
> Their music goes out through all the earth,
>     their words reach to the end of the world.
>
> (PSALM 19:1–4, NEB)

The music of God, the word of God, spoken, communicated through the furthest stars, through the radar of the bat, the invisible wires drawing the homing pigeon.

In such a way all things began. The book of Genesis records how, in the beginning of creation when God made heaven and earth, the earth was without form and void. God spoke, the word of God communicated. "Let there be light" – and there was light. The communication of God was, and is, through and in all things. All things are interrelated. We can look in each other's eyes and without a word communicate love, fear, sorrow. By the touch of a hand we can give each other comfort, pain, applause. God is between all things – what Bishop John Taylor called "the Go-between God".

It is one of the great deprivations of modern humans that we allow ourselves so little silence. As we allow silence to invade us, we can be part of, swim in, this stream of sounds and signs, and find God's harmony and wonder in our silence. As we listen to our breathing or the wind in the trees, we wonder about God, what sort of God it is out there, in here. The starlings are vicious and greedy, the swallows are weeded out on their flight and only the strong survive, the cells of my brain are decaying, the loving hands can turn into fists, the eyes can be pornographic. There is a frightening ambiguity, the Word of God in nature and human beings seems to be badly tuned. There is serious interference – the crackling of our own noise, the distortion of our own fear and selfishness, means we cannot hear and see God in the beauty of Holiness. For all we know, God may be warlike Mars, a nuclear enthusiast, cruel, remote. What sort of God lies beyond our silence? Through our history, mankind has wanted to appease Him, looking on towards death with anxious, unknowing, unseeing eyes. God unknown, unknowable. What sort of composer is this God?

The God of nature is not enough. The music of the universe is like all great music − full of passion, of conflict, of peace, of storms and deep lakes and aweful mountains. But is God just a neutral force? Are we just part of the process − a moment in a tragic comedy, a small cell amongst a billion billion, without meaning and destiny?

The being and action of God are communicated throughout the whole created order and, for the Christian, through Jesus. St John has brought together this Creator God and Jesus Christ through the use of "the Word", the *Logos*. Believing and trusting in the Father who made all things, St John sees the Word as the agent of that outpouring which was and is God's act of creation:

> When all things began, the Word already was. The Word dwelt with God, and what God was, the Word was. The Word, then, was with God at the beginning, and through him all things came to be; no single thing was created without him. All that came to be was alive with his life, and that life was the light of men . . . The real light which enlightens every man was even then coming into the world. (JOHN 1:1−4, 9)

The light of God in every human soul was drawn from the Word and this Word became human in Christ:

> So the Word became flesh; he came to dwell among us, and we saw his glory, such glory as befits the Father's only Son, full of grace and truth. (JOHN 1:14)

The invisible God came into the world which He had created:

> He was in the world; but the world, though it owed its being to him, did not recognize him. He entered his own realm, and his own would not receive him. (JOHN 1:10–11)

God in His greatness remained a vast transcendent mystery, but in Christ we see what we need to know of His nature and His purpose. Jesus is the human face of the Word. Seeing His face does not reduce the wonder and splendour of the Godness of God, but rather focuses in human form what we need to know of God's intentions. His intentions are hinted at, and indeed stated, many times in the psalter – in the use of the word "*Hesed*" – the merciful loving-kindness of God (Psalm 136); in terms of the forgiveness of God (in Psalm 103); and in the love of God (in Psalm 139); and the suffering of His servant (in Psalm 22). For the Christian, Christ is the human communication of the being of God.

> He is the image of the invisible God; his is the primacy over all created things. In him everything in heaven and on earth was created, not only things visible but also the invisible orders of thrones, sovereignties, authorities, and powers: the whole universe has been created through him and for him. And he exists before everything, and all things are held together in him . . . For in him the complete being of God, by God's own choice, came to dwell. (COLOSSIANS 1:15–17, 19)

The theme, the purpose of the music of God is a love like Christ's. "My song is love unknown" – the word, the music that ripples through all created things. The word is love — not sentimental nor marshmallow, but powerful, suffering, crying, laughing, dying. The purpose and the theme are love. That is why the Mass, the Gospel, the struggle with evil and suffering and the resurrection have for centuries filled the souls of musicians who are seeking a clue to the song of the universal God. A Man of Sorrows, acquainted with grief — but through His love a final chorus of all the saints, of angels and archangels singing, "Glory to God in the highest, peace to his people on earth." So in the music, in the silence of our lives, we can experience in prayer, in meditation, in adoring, the mystery of God, the great unfinished symphony.

\*　\*　\*　\*　\*

*You send springs into the gullies:*
*which run between the hills;*
*they give drink to every beast of the field:*
*and the wild asses quench their thirst.*
*Beside them the birds of the air build their nests:*
*and sing among the branches.*
*You water the mountains from your dwelling on high:*
*and the earth is filled by the fruits of your work.*
*You cause the grass to grow for the cattle:*
*and all green things for the servants of mankind.*
*You bring food out of the earth:*
*and wine that makes glad the heart of man,*
*oil to give him a shining countenance:*
*and bread to strengthen his heart.*
*The trees of the Lord are well watered:*

> *the cedars of Lebanon that he has planted,*
> *where the birds build their nests:*
> *and the stork makes her home in the pine-tops.*
> *The high hills are a refuge for the wild goats:*
> *and the crags a cover for the conies.*
> . . . .
> *These all look to you:*
> *to give them their food in due season.*
> *When you give it to them they gather it:*
> *when you open your hand they are satisfied with*
>    *good things.*

As I write this meditation in the warm sunshine in the Garden of England, the abundant provision of God is around me everywhere I look. The branches of the apple trees gently drop their fruit into the waiting basket, the damsons and plums wait for the nimble hands. Two small boys throw the windfalls at each other, the rams will soon race through the fields of ewes and before Easter there will be single, twin, triplet lambs slithering into life. The earth swarms with being:

> *Lord how various are your works:*
> *. . . the earth is full of your creatures.*
> *There is the wide immeasurable sea:*
> *there move living things without number*
> . . .
> *These all look to you:*
> *to give them their food in due season.*
> *When you give it to them they gather it:*
> *when you open your hand they are*
>    *satisfied with good things.*

To the people of the psalter this immediate sense of God providing the plenty they required to live was not obscured by the supermarket mentality. They saw the whole process through – from the sowing to the reaping, the threshing, the grinding and the baking. If it rained, they had plenty, and if it did not, they went hungry. So the harvest thanksgiving was a time of great rejoicing when all the people gave thanks to God for the wonderful provision He had made.

All this bounty only emphasized the loving-kindness of God who made them, and became a further cause of blessing. So it was part of their whole way of looking at life to thank and praise God, expressing in song their gratitude:

> You tend the earth and water it:
> you make it rich and fertile.
> The river of God is full of water:
> and so providing for the earth
>     you provide grain for men.
> You drench its furrows, you level the
>     ridges between:
> you soften it with showers and bless its
>     early growth.
> You crown the year with your goodness:
> and the tracks where you have passed
>     drip with fatness.
> The pastures of the wilderness run over:
> and the hills are girded with joy.
> The meadows are clothed with sheep:
> and the valleys stand so thick with corn
> they shout for joy and sing.

> (PSALM 65:8–13)

For them there was a direct link between their food and drink and God who gave it:

> *You cause the grass to grow for the cattle:*
> *and all green things for the servants of mankind.*
> *You bring food out of the earth:*
> *and wine that makes glad the heart of man,*
> *oil to give him a shining countenance:*
> *and bread to strengthen his heart.*

There was a match between need and supply in God's world as he made it – an ecology of creation. We are a long way from this clear and distinct understanding, losing sight of the source of our food and drink and prosperity, and frequently distorting and damaging the garden we have been given. We are a generation with battery hens and acid rain, a generation of unparalleled production and unparalleled famine – of swollen supplies and swollen children's bellies. We seem to have lost our reverence for the received earth and its plenty. We eliminate its species, we mass-slaughter its whales, we waste prodigious quantities of food. This is a sickness of our age, the gross wickedness which derives from our greed and our competitiveness combined with our ingenuity and lack of wisdom. Hosea said of the people of Israel: "For she does not know that it is [God] who gave her corn, new wine and oil" (HOSEA 2:8). Because Israel did not recognize that the Lord gave the plenty she enjoyed, so her hunger was never to be satisfied – always thirsting for more: "They shall eat but never be satisfied, behave wantonly but their lust will never be overtaxed." (HOSEA 4:10)

I can recognize such blindness in myself and in society

around me. We have mostly stopped saying Grace at meals, which was the basic reminder that it is God who gives the plenty. With our desire to produce more and more and to build up our wealth irrespective of our creator or the justice He demands, we are a little deranged, and miss out on the thanksgiving. I said Grace at a huge business dinner with five courses, four different wines, and ate and drank my fill. But I could not sleep that night — not just because of my rather unreliable digestive system, but because the Grace seemed, for most of the people there, a meaningless anachronism. We are makers of our destiny, the great creators, manufacturers, creators of wealth — in no way the humble stewards of the plenty of God. This basic disharmony with God is responsible for our refusal to tackle the hunger and desperate erosion of the goodness of the soil, polluting and consuming at breakneck speed the natural treasures of His world. It is against this terrifying reality that Psalm 104 reminds us of God's ecology, where we work humbly to co-operate with the system he has created:

> *You created the moon to mark the seasons:*
> *and the sun knows the hour of its setting.*
> *You make darkness and it is night:*
> *in which all the beasts of the forest move by stealth.*
> *The lions roar for their prey:*
> *seeking their food from God.*
> *When the sun rises they retire:*
> *and lay themselves down in their dens.*
> *Man goes out to his work:*
> *and to his labour until the evening.*

In Psalm 72, there is a direct link made between the justice of the nations and the promise of God. The psalmist prays that the king will

> judge your people rightly:
> and the poor of the land with equity.
> . . . rescue the children of the needy
> and crush the oppressor.

The prayer is repeated:

> He will deliver the needy when they cry:
> and the poor man that has no helper.
> He will pity the helpless and the needy:
> and save the lives of the poor.
> He will redeem them from oppression and
>     violence:
> and their blood shall be precious in his sight.

If the king and the people will only live according to the will of God, the plenty of God will follow:

> Let there be abundance of wheat in the land:
> let it flourish on the tops of the mountains.
>                    (Psalm 72:2,4,12–14,16)

We need to discover a new reverence for His creation. The people who shared in the cult in the Temple were reminded of the source of their plenty – the one who gave them life and sustenance. To forget God or turn against Him is to distort our image of the earth in which we live, to fracture its links and to undermine its wholeness.

*     *     *     *     *

*May the glory of the Lord endure for ever:*
*may the Lord rejoice in his works.*
*If he look upon the earth it shall tremble:*
*if he but touch the mountains they shall smoke.*

If you believe in God, it is not long before you ask, "What does God think of me?" and "What does He think of the whole human race?" Shame follows hard on the heels of these questions. "Woe is me! I am lost, for I am a man of unclean lips and I dwell among a people of unclean lips" (Isaiah 6:5). It is bad enough to think of what the people we love would think if they knew everything we had ever done. When each of my own loved ones have died – my mother-in-law, my mother, my father – I have struggled with the thought that now they know everything about me, and this leads to a sense of shame, amongst all the other feelings and thoughts associated with them. How much more awesome is the thought of God's thoughts about me and His world. Maybe this sense of shame is a healthy experience if it doesn't get us bogged down in guilt. God's aweful wonder is expressed over and over again in the Bible. The birth of shame is described in Genesis:

The man and his wife heard the sound of the Lord God walking in the garden at the time of the evening breeze and hid from the Lord God among the trees of the garden. But the Lord God called to the man and said to him, "Where are you?" He replied, "I heard the sound as you were walking in the garden, and I was afraid because I was naked, and I hid myself." (GENESIS 3:8–10)

This is the sense of our own absurdity when we look up towards the infinite God whose holiness cannot be gazed upon and whose judgement reduces us to nothing. Moses walks up the mountain of God and a bush burns with the heat of the presence of God. The Red Sea is thrown up into great walls by the power of God. The Ark of God brings death to all who touch it. Psalm 29 bids the worshippers recall the awful mystery of God. As they come to the temple their hearts are beating faster:

> Ascribe to the Lord the honour due to his name:
> O worship the Lord in the beauty of his holiness.
> The voice of the Lord is upon the waters:
> the God of glory thunders
> the Lord upon the great waters.
> The voice of the Lord is mighty in operation:
> the voice of the Lord is a glorious voice.
> The voice of the Lord breaks the cedar-trees:
> The Lord breaks in pieces the cedars of
> Lebanon.

> (PSALM 29:2–5)

When all Job's arguments are done and he is finally lost for words, God utters His aweful judgment out of the storm:

> Who is this whose ignorant words
> cloud my design in darkness?
> Brace yourself and stand up like a man;
> I will ask questions, and you shall answer.
> Where were you when I laid the earth's foundations?
> Tell me, if you know and understand.

Who settled its dimensions? Surely you should know.

(JOB 38:2-5)

Compared with the immensity and power of God, Job can only answer:

> I know that thou canst do all things
> and that no purpose is beyond thee.
> but I have spoken of great things which I have not
>     understood,
> things too wonderful for me to know.
> I knew of thee then only by report,
> but now I see thee with my own eyes.
> Therefore I melt away;
> I repent in dust and ashes. (JOB 42:2-6)

This is a hard and fearful place to leave us. We fear so much, we carry a great deal of shame and are threatened all the time with insignificance: "What is man that you should be mindful of him?" (PSALM 8:5), and it is here that the revelation of Christ makes such a difference to us who believe.

We stand before God who has revealed His nature and purpose in Christ. The awefulness of God is subject to His love. "To crown all there must be love", and that love casts out the fear. The experience of Christ for St Paul was an experience of freedom and forgiveness before almighty God. The awefulness and the holiness of God were no longer a threat to annihilate him, but a source of loving power in his life. The contemporary Christian often forgets the otherness, the awefulness, the immensity, the power of God — and so we reduce our understanding. But when we do ponder His majesty, the incredible creation, we do so in remembrance of His son who came to visit us in great humility. Our worship and our approach to life should stand at the great gates of the eternal truth that Christ is seated at the right hand of the Father, that all His love and acceptance and affirmation of us, are a perfect reflection of God.

So the psalm draws to an end. The prayer has led the psalmist to the point of exaltation:

> *I will sing to the Lord as long as I live:*
> *I will praise my God while I have any being.*

It is not easy to describe the joy which can be experienced in the worship of God. It can be known in Haggerston and Toxteth, in Brixton and Gerrard's Cross, when the human heart and mind are opened to the wonder of God and catch a hint of the eternal glory which shines through the gate of heaven. Then, in one of those vertigo plunges we see in the psalms, there is a postscript about sinners (v37a). Perhaps we can recognize the psalmist's longing that sin and wickedness will be no more – but recognize only too clearly that we are sinners too. But this side-swipe only delays him a moment, and finally the great burst of love wells up within him:

> *Bless the Lord O my soul*
> *O praise the Lord.*

# PSALM 137
## How Shall We Sing the
## Lord's Song in a Strange Land?

By the waters of Babylon we sat down and wept:
when we remembered Zion.

As for our harps we hung them up:
upon the trees that are in that land.

For there those who led us away captive
required of us a song:
and those who had despoiled us demanded mirth
saying, "Sing us one of the songs of Zion."

How can we sing the Lord's song in a strange land?

If I forget you O Jerusalem:
let my right hand forget its mastery.

Let my tongue cling to the roof of my mouth:
if I do not remember you
if I do not prefer Jerusalem above my chief joy.

Remember O Lord against the Edomites
the day of Jerusalem
how they said, "Down with it, down with it,
raze it to its foundations."

O daughter of Babylon, you that lay waste:
happy shall he be who serves you as you have served us;

*happy shall he be who takes your little ones:*
*and dashes them against the stones.*

Much of my ministry has been involved with exiles, people who are treated as aliens – immigrants, the disabled, the homeless, gay people, the lonely, prisoners, the unloved. I don't know why this should be except that I have myself been loved so much more than I deserve, and even so I know something of what it feels to be an exile. In our experience of exile we come close to Jesus, who described himself in these terms: "Foxes have their holes, the birds their roosts, but the son of Man has nowhere to lay his head" (MATTHEW 8:20). In the end he was put to death outside the city.

It is a mystery that the people of God should have been subjected so often to oppression, to being carried away into exile, to exodus and return. It is a recurring story of the Old Testament. This psalm expresses the cry of the exiles who in their slavery are cut off from their home. Although it is a song of Israel, it is also a universal song – a longing for peace in which the Lord's song can be sung without fear.

To this psalm belongs the distinction of being Number One on "Top Of The Pops". A singing group called Boney M recorded this song in the 1970s. They presented a glamorous image of sequins and glitter. It was a great hit and remains a favourite. I don't know what this song meant to them in their own minds, but the gold and silver shiny wrapping they gave it contrasted sharply with the agony of the psalm itself. Perhaps they had reflected upon the history of slavery, the uprooting of the African peoples by tyrant traders, and the desperate cruelty of wrenching a people out of their setting, their sacred places and customs, their homeland. Perhaps they saw in their imagination the sailors chaining the slaves together in the hold of a ship and selling them out of their tribal way of life into the humiliation, the dehumanization of a life of forced labour as a possession amongst other possessions. For the first slaves, their captivity must have been a stunning intrusion in their ideas of holiness – beautifully expressed in the story of Kunta Kinte in *Roots*. Perhaps Boney M thought of all this, or perhaps they sang more than they knew. This psalm – this song – must have been a comfort, an expression of grief and faith – not only for Jews through the ages, but for every oppressed and exiled people who have sung it.

The original composer of this lament was either describing his own experience or was vividly imagining and reliving the experience of his ancestors. At least we know something of the events and the setting which the composer describes.

The singers and the musicians in the Temple had a special place in the worship, and were jealous of their rights and privileges. They were important because they sang the story of God's people and expressed the worship on behalf of the congregation, who would respond to the words with shouts of acclamation. "The singers did not recite or sing in the Temple 'at sight', they had to know the psalms by heart and teach them to their sons – and the psalms became the inheritance of the singers' families."[1] Mowinckel includes this in his fascinating description of the way in which the singers became a sort of guild who were in the lower ranks of the hereditary orders. The nearest contemporary parallel is a cathedral choir and musicians, knowing the songs by heart, passing on the tradition from generation to generation. A glimpse of something not unknown in the cathedrals of our day could be gained from Mowinckel's comment, "We have evidence also of the existence of strained and antagonistic relations between singers and priests"!

But the Temple singers and musicians did not live in the security of a free society, because Jerusalem had been overrun by conquering forces so many times. "Sennacherib, in his account of the siege of Jerusalem, states that Hezekiah sent 'male and female musicians' as part of his tribute." [2] Then, when in 587 BC Jerusalem fell into the hands of the Babylonian conquerors, there is no doubt that singers and musicians would have been taken into exile too. It is therefore likely that this poem was written by a Temple singer who himself had been in exile, or who was the son or descendant of some such singer. The poem has all the power of personal experience still in its veins. The Temple was in ruins, and when the exiles and their children and their children's children returned, they found the city had been further damaged, looted and destroyed by their ancient enemies and neighbours. As the psalmist recalls the humiliation of deportation, and the despair of his destroyed city, he expresses rage and cries out to God for revenge. As we work through the psalm we shall find that the singer was singing a song for all ages and many peoples who have been refugees, slaves, deportees, aliens, homeless and oppressed. It is a universal song speaking from the grief of mankind, and therefore a song which can touch us also.

\* \* \* \* \*

## Psalm 137

*By the rivers of Babylon we sat down and wept when we remembered Zion.*

To us, Babylon is just the name of an ancient city in Persia (now Iran), but for the composer it conjured up a time and a place of terror and violence, of total alienation. The people were in exile there many years, and had to find a way of surviving, of settling and, in the midst of this enemy territory, finding a way of life. In 1945 it was hard enough for displaced persons in and after the Second World War to build a new life in a friendly country – how much more difficult it would have been to be deported to Dresden or Frankfurt if Hitler had been victorious. How the prisoners of all wars must have longed for their homeland, for the familiar, domestic scene. It is not difficult for us to imagine the pain of "remembering Zion". The Jews in all their dispersion and suffering have remembered Zion – the place where they hope they will experience no alienation of spirit. Perhaps we all have our own Zion where we will be at peace in our environment, in our way of life and our worship of God.

We do not have to be deported to experience alienation. It is possible to an exile, an alien, in our own home. I remember travelling in a Land Rover from Mombasa to Johannesburg. We stayed in several homes where we were told that the black servants were untrustworthy, where the white lady of the house carried a large bunch of keys and locked every cupboard. Then we arrived at the home of Garfield and Grace Todd in Southern Rhodesia (as it then was). There we experienced a new multi-racial joy with its laughter and its hope. Yet the house was often a target of raids, and they locked the cupboards when the white police arrived. Garfield was held in detention for long periods, and was treated by many of his white contemporaries as an alien in their midst – yet he was so wonderfully "at home" with the people who were to become Zimbabwe. One of the South African blasphemies is the use of the expression "the homelands", to describe the places of exile created for black people. It takes one of the precious needs of all human beings and turns it into an excuse to deport people, separate families and reduce people to poverty.

But it is not just in Africa and Communist countries and Palestine and the other places of oppression and deportation and displacement of peoples that alienation and exile are experienced. We have our own less obvious and dramatic examples. There is the rather refined and painful experience of being the Outsider: "Mother died today. Or maybe yesterday. I can't be sure."[3] It is an experience of unreality and disconnection. When I was a young man, it looked like a luxury of the well-off to agonize about the loss of meaning and purpose in life. But since that time I have seen so much mental illness and become increasingly aware of the alienation from society caused by being poor and deprived in a glittering and affluent society. Near my home there are people who have been alienated or have alienated themselves and whose grief is obvious. Four men live in a house and every morning set out to the off-licence and then spend the day drinking themselves into a foreign place where their senses are distorted and where they become disconnected. Again, a young fifteen-year-old boy hid an aerosol of lighter fuel in our front garden. He is in care and sniffs six aerosols a day. His alienation began when his mother and father went through the stages of marriage breakdown and created a boy who had no one to trust, nowhere to be truly at home. At another home there are a family of brothers and sisters who have not been able to find work and who have discovered their own alternative life-style which alienates them from law-abiding society and makes the streets into a battleground with the police. I have seen a husband become an exile from his house because his wife has a lover who has moved in, and I have met mothers who are cut off from all social life and become trapped in their flat – disconnected from the warmth and companionship which make life worth while. There is a little old lady who walks the streets of Mile End, visits the local mental hospital and spends most of the rest of her time gazing out of her window – knowing no one, speaking with no one – an exile. The owners sold the house and the builders moved in. They put up scaffolding and gutted it – and the lady still walked into the house up to "her" room and looked out of the glassless window with unseeing eyes.

In many of these stories the tragedy is that they have no Zion to remember, no place of harmony and peace. Harvey Cox praised the anonymity of the Secular City because it gave the person of independent means and cultural riches an opportunity for privacy – the dedicated pursuit of their own fascinating lives – but the anonymity of the city can be for others the source of daily desolation in which the privacy becomes a trap and the anonymity becomes a loss of identity. People who are never named become people who are not recognized, who are not affirmed. I have seen this exile become so serious that a person begins to doubt they exist at all. "I hadn't any right to exist. I had appeared by chance, I existed like a stone, a plant, a microbe."[4]

There is a good deal of weeping in our city, and many exiles. Once I visited with Bangladeshi friends a flat in East India Buildings where burning rags had been put through the letter box, where windows had been broken and where the family dared not go out of the flat for fear of assault. We set about visiting all the flats in the block; it opened doors of families and individuals of all races who were experiencing suffering and deprivation of every kind. The place was surrounded by scaffolding which had been there for months and months to improve the property – but the money ran out, and the scaffolding remained, granting immediate accesss to intruders. The anger at the lack of official or comunity response to their dreadful insecurity turned and was expressed in anger against the poor black people who shared their predicament. Since that time we have seen families made homeless sitting in a church hall – totally exiled from normal life, with nowhere to lay their head.

The Jewish community has learned from millennia of experience what it is like to be aliens and exiles, and they have developed a corporate and mutual responsibility which has enabled them to survive, and indeed thrive. Because of their own experience of slavery, of deportation and persecution, they have been able to resist the tyrant powers by mutual support, and their faith teaches them how to treat the foreigners in their community: "You shall not wrong an alien, or be hard upon him; you were yourselves aliens in Egypt'' (EXODUS 22:21). This deep tradition makes the current tragic alienation of the Palestinians seem such a denial of Israel's purpose before God.

The battle against alienation should be a central feature of the Church's life too, because Christ was someone who reached out to the aliens and included them. The leper was touched, the traitorous tax-gatherer was embraced, the adulteress saved from death by stoning. He was accused of associating with those who were exiled from the holy people, he died with sinners. But it is not just because Christ included the outsiders, but also because the Christian, like the Jew, has been included by God. Our sins, our pathetic failures, our fearful selfishness, turn us away from God, and by His forgiveness and love we have been brought home to Zion: "You are now the people of God, who once were not his people: outside his mercy once, you have now received his mercy" (1 PETER 2:10).

We forgive because we have been forgiven; we should welcome and include others because we have been welcomed and included by God. This has profound importance – not just for our behaviour as individuals, as neighbours or colleagues, but for our society. We see some encouraging demonstrations of this "including people in" – where decent accommodation is built for homeless people, where disabled people are received, accepted and given a task. We see it also where racial discrimination is lost in the pleasure and richness of multi-racial life, where we take what has been learned on the sports field into all the walks and ranks of life. The Christian who is drenched in the word of God cannot help but work for and with those minorities in the community who have been excluded and alienated. It is possible that in the next ten years we shall create a whole alienated class, what Professor Dahrendorf called "an underclass", who will be exiled from the opportunity to work, to have a decent home and, above all, prevented from contributing to the community and the society to which they should belong.

The Church is often accused of entering the political debate. The Church of England report *Faith in the City* brought down upon us the wrath of those who thought we were interfering in matters which were not our concern. But if you pray the psalms every day, you realize that justice, the care of the poor, the wholeness of society are all involved in God's purpose. The alien, the fatherless and the widow should constantly be on the mind of the Christian as of the Jew, because we have been saved from our own exile and alienation from God. To those of us who struggle with alienated places and try to reach alientated people, these are matters of daily experience. Like Ezekiel, we live where it hurts and our prayers and the songs of our salvation constantly lead us to try and tackle the exile and alienation of people where they weep:

> So I came to the exiles at Tel-abib who were settled by the river Kebar. For seven days I stayed with them, dumbfounded. (EZEKIEL 3:15)

> In the course of a series of visits we saw something of the physical conditions under which people in the Urban Priority Areas are living and we listened to their own accounts and experiences at open public meeings and in smaller invited groups. (*Faith in the City*)[5]

We are called to share in the Restoration of Zion – not in the sense of the state of Israel, but the new Jerusalem, where God reigns.

Although the new Jerusalem is to be the great act of God, and although our efforts and yearnings look so puny and ineffective, nevertheless God restores our energy and motivation and will not allow us to become like those who seemingly accept the degradation and injustice which exist on the earth.

St Augustine saw Babylon and Jerusalem in a different way: ". . . there are two cities, for the present outwardly mingled together, yet separated in heart, running together through the course of time until the end; one whose end is everlasting peace, and it is called Jerusalem; the other whose joy is peace in this world, and it is called Babylon."[6]

However, St Augustine's negative view of the earth contrasts with Isaiah's vision of the new creation which could hardly have a stronger scent of the soil:

> For behold, I create
> new heavens and a new earth.
> > Former things shall no more be remembered
> > nor shall they be called to mind.
> > Rejoice and be filled with delight,
> > you boundless realms which I create;
> for I create Jerusalem to be a delight
> > and her people a joy;
> I will take delight in Jerusalem and rejoice in my
> people;
> > weeping and cries for help

shall never again be heard in her.
There no child shall ever again die an infant,
  no old man fail to live out his life;
    every boy shall live his hundred years before he
    dies,
whoever falls short of a hundred shall be despised.
  Men shall build houses and live to inhabit them,
plant vineyards and eat their fruit;
  . . .
The wolf and the lamb shall feed together
and the lion shall eat straw like the cattle.
They shall not hurt or destroy in all my holy mountain,
  says the Lord. (ISAIAH 65:17–21, 25)

I like to think of the Kingdom of God as breaking through
into our world whenever we love God — so that the world
may be enjoyed when we are in harmony with Him. But
the way of the Kingdom may lead us to suffering and
struggle, and then we must not choose the comfort rather
than His justice and truth. The new creation begins wherever
God reigns in us and we catch a glimpse of the place of
peace. Babylon symbolizes the oppressor and the seducer,
and in our search for the everlasting city we have to choose
the liberty and the love of the children of God.

The singers and the musicians took into exile their
knowledge and their skill. Their trade was to sing the songs
of Zion and accompany them on the harp and lyre and
drum. Their memory of life in the Temple is conjured up
by the words from another psalm.

  Your procession is seen O God:
  the procession of my God and King in the sanctuary.

The singers go before, the musicians come after:
and around them the maidens beating on the timbrels.
In their choirs they bless God:
those that are sprung from the fount of Israel
bless the Lord. (PSALM 68:24–6)

But in exile, their captors mocked them and taunted them,
calling on them to sing the songs for their entertainment.
But they were members of a defeated and deported people,
their song spoke of the power and loving-kindness of their
God. How could they sing these words which had echoed
round the Temple in days gone by?

I was glad when they said to me:
"Let us go to the house of the Lord."
And now our feet are standing:
within your gates O Jerusalem;
Jerusalem which is built as a city:
where the pilgrims gather in unity.
There the tribes go up, the tribes of the Lord:
as he commanded Israel
to give thanks to the name of the Lord.
There are set thrones of judgement:
the thrones of the house of David.
O pray for the peace of Jerusalem:
may those who love you prosper.
peace be within your walls:
and prosperity in your palaces.
For the sake of my brothers and companions:
I will pray that peace be with you.
For the sake of the house of the Lord our God:
I will seek for your good. (PSALM 122)

The Temple was in ruins, the people of Israel divided and defeated, and this implied something worse – that they themselves were under the judgement of God. They were exiled because of what they had done as the people of God. If God rewarded righteousness and goodness and obedience, then they had been exiled because they were disobedient and unclean. They were a disobedient and unclean people amongst foreigners in a strange land. They could not sing their songs except to lament and wait and pray for the deliverance of God. They believed God was in control of history, and therefore their tragedy was a punishment. All they could do was to try to live a blameless life and plead with God to free them. The psalmists often reminded God forcefully of the promise He had made, the covenant with them He had agreed. They would now see it as a betrayal to sing the Lord's song in their captivity for entertainment – it would be a blasphemy. It is a common feature of life that people who experience tragedy assume that it is punishment of their wrong-doing, often at the hand of God. It may, of course, be the result of our behaviour, but often it is not. It is difficult to imagine a loving God using cancer or starvation as a punishment – and if we could imagine Him, He would be unacceptable and subhuman.

It is not surprising that the pictures of the concentration camps come into the conscious mind sometimes when reading this psalm. There is the true story of a musician in an orchestra commanded to play whilst victims were taken to the gas chambers. The singers can tell of the sorrows of exile and the hope of return as an expression of the feelings and longings of the slaves – but not to sing the Lord's song as entertainment, to add insult to injury. Their captors called on them to be merry, but there was only grief.

Again the sharpness of the poet's imagery evokes not only the sorrow of the harpist and singers, but takes us into a far wider experience of the people of faith. This psalm has sometimes seemed directly applicable to my own ministry and the ministry of my colleagues. In my twenty years as a priest, it has been nicely assumed that we are a Christian country. The Queen is head of the Church of England. Our senior bishops sit in the House of Lords. We have a parish church in every place in the land. We are called the Church of England. There have been many times when I have felt the cold draught of deep antipathy to the Gospel as we understand it and seek to proclaim it. It took me some time to realize that the combined Christian presence was a minority view in this country, and that whilst many people have a vague allegiance to Christianity it is not an allegiance sharpened, refreshed, inspired by worship or the Scriptures or regular prayer. All sorts of assumptions about justice, about family life, about work, are made on the basis of a sort of general Christian view, but it is only too easy to be brought up sharply by the increasing gap between society's assumptions and the faith we proclaim.

The first time I led a Good Friday service there were twenty people in a church which could hold two thousand, and at roughly the same time more than thirty thousand were watching West Ham play their Good Friday football match. My feelings were strong and I could say with the psalmist, "How can I sing the Lord's song?". The Church is, of course, in part responsible in a whole range of ways, but it also has to be faced that there is an incredibly wide gap between the Gospel of Christ and the ways and attitudes of our society. We cannot assume a Christian culture, and we therefore have to expect more enmity against the views we hold. Sometimes I buy a wide range of papers and I see Christians described as communists, as faithless, as ignorant, as naïve and "trendy". The delight at catching out a vicar in a compromising situation has a degree of nastiness which did not mark the old jokes about the bishop and the actress. There's an element of "There you are — we told you". We are accused of not giving a moral lead, and have even been blamed for society's troubles — in spite of the fact that for the twenty years I have been a priest I have been, with my colleagues, attempting day in day out to sing the Lord's song in a strange land and tell of His commandments. I could write a book on this profound divergence, but must satisfy myself with one or two examples.

We could take the contemporary image of the successful person as portrayed in newspapers, in television advertising, in incentive policies, and compare that glossy image with the vision of humanness portrayed by Christ and described by St Paul:

My brothers, think what sort of people you are, whom God has called. Few of you are men of wisdom, by any human standard; few are powerful or highly born. Yet, to shame the wise, God has chosen what the world counts folly, and to shame what is strong, God has chosen what the world counts weakness. He has chosen things low and contemptible, mere nothings, to overthrow the existing order. (1 CORINTHIANS 1:26–8)

Or consider our investment in material advancement. The Bible is materialistic in the sense that it recognizes that we have material needs, and indeed fiercely condemns those who bring down poverty on others. Yet the most repeated theme of the Old and New Testaments is that salvation and fullness of life do not consist of riches or material possessions at all. It is an irony of today that those who possess most are those who claim and insist that the failings of the poor of society are due to the lack of spiritual attitudes. Jesus said, Blessed are you poor." Mary said, "The rich he has sent empty away." The out-and-out materialist risks his soul.

> We brought nothing into the world; for that matter we cannot take anything with us when we leave, but if we have food and covering we may rest content. Those who want to be rich fall into temptations and snares and many foolish harmful desires which plunge men into ruin and perdition. The love of money is the root of all evil things, and there are some who in reaching for it have wandered from the faith and spiked themselves on many thorny griefs. (1 TIMOTHY 6:7–10)

But like the rich young ruler, the rich go away sorrowing because they prefer the solace of captivity.

Or again, in the face of sexual permissiveness, the Church has clung desperately to its belief about fidelity in human relationships – trying to cope with the anger of the divorced, the scorn of the young and the apparent "freedom" created by the Pill. Yet we are accused of being the cause of the widespread infidelity, the broken marriages and the breakdown of family life. Ours is no easy Gospel to proclaim in this land, and the Church and her priests and leaders are made the scapegoats of the clear worship of other gods by many of our citizens, expressed daily by their newspapers.

There have been many times that Christian men have been afraid to speak up about their faith in their working environment because for some reason faith in this country is not seen to be manly. Perhaps that is because of the offensive image of masculinity which has been the disastrous propaganda of a "macho" age. Jesus had no wife, no home, no possessions, was opposed to violence, expressed tenderness, cared with a powerful compassion and promised peace as his parting gift. It is difficult to link this image to the "bovver boy", the "history man", and the womanizer.

There have certainly been times in my years as a priest when I have moved too quickly with a fashionable belief, but there have always been Scripture and tradition to raise the questions, to unsettle the false new certainties, and make me hesitate until the new understanding has been tested. It has been at least as common a fault of religious people that they have refused to change in the light of experience, as though God switched off the light of His Holy Spirit in the year the Bible was completed. We now totally accept changes which in the past have been the subject of great battles in the Church. We do not regard menstruation as making a woman unclean, we do not stone people to death, we do not sacrifice animals, we do not believe the world was made in seven days. Some of these changes caused great difficulties for the Church, but have eventually been accepted. So we have to explore in each generation what the Spirit is saying to the Churches now in the light of the Scriptures and the tradition. When pioneers fight for some change of understanding, they will no doubt be accused, like the first Christians, of being atheists. We must not be tempted to hang up our harp, yet we must at the same time resist the idea that the Lord's song is just another form of entertainment to go along with quiz games, bingo and football pools. Nor must the Gospel preaching give tacit approval to, or collude with, injustice. We need a large dose of hope and guts drawn from the Spirit of God to stand for the Gospel view of people and society. There are still Christian roots in good trees that grow even where the roots are hidden. I think society may be like the Jewish taxi driver I described earlier in this book, who secretly longed for the truths of the God his mother believed in, yet could not bring himself to the synagogue. We have to work against our becoming "a strange land" by finding our allies wherever they are, supporting those outside the Church who witness to the good and the right, and by firmly restating and, above all, living out the Lord's Song as we see it.

* * * * *

> *If I forget you O Jerusalem:*
> *let my right hand forget its mastery.*
> *Let my tongue cling to the roof of my mouth*
> *if I do not remember you*
> *if I do not prefer Jerusalem above my chief joy.*

Our poem now moves into the present tense. The psalmist has been looking back to the exile — recalling terrible times. Now his song turns to Jerusalem as it is. What he sees moves him to deep passion. He feels a great and all-consuming love and longing for Jerusalem to be restored. He curses himself if ever he were to let Jeruslaem down. "Let my right hand forget its mastery. Let my tongue cling to the roof of my mouth" was a curse threatening his whole life and livelihood as a musician or singer. He curses himself if he does not "prefer Jerusalem above my chief joy". Words were thought of as having great power for good or evil. Blessings and curses abounded and were believed to be effective in themselves. This self-cursing is no light matter, and the well-being of Jerusalem is now to be his highest goal. When Jesus came near to Jerusalem, he wept over it: "O Jerusalem, Jerusalem . . . How often have I longed to gather your children, as a hen gathers her brood under her wings; but you would not let me" (MATTHEW 23:37). Although the faithful Jew believes that the Lord makes His dwelling-place wherever the Torah is recited and not just in Jerusalem, Zionism has been and remains a powerful force in the world – a zeal derived not only from the love of the city of God, but also from the myriad experiences of persecution and anti-Semitism. Though the Christian can love Jerusalem, make pilgrimage and revere the seat of David and the streets that led to Calvary, there is obviously a new vision brought about by the death of Christ. With the death of Jesus comes the death of the specific earthly locality of God. The vision shifts from Israel and Jerusalem to the new Israel and the new Jerusalem – the eternal city.

Then I saw a new heaven and a new earth, for the first heaven and the first earth had vanished, and there was no longer any sea. I saw the holy city, new Jerusalem, coming down out of heaven from God, made ready like a bride adorned for her husband. I heard a loud voice proclaiming from the throne: "Now at last God has his dwelling among men! He will dwell among them and they shall be his people, and God himself will be with them. He will wipe every tear from their eyes; there shall be an end to death, and to mourning and crying and pain; for the old order has passed away!" (REVELATION 21:1–4)

The old Temple will be superseded. The Samaritan woman said to Jesus: "Our fathers worshipped on this mountain, but you Jews say that the temple where God should be worshipped is in Jerusalem." Jesus directed her beyond locality to a new dwelling place of God:

> . . . the time is coming when you will worship the Father neither on this mountain, nor in Jerusalem . . . But the time approaches, indeed it is already here, when those who are real worshippers will worship the Father in spirit and in truth. Such are the worshippers whom the Father wants. God is spirit, and those who worship him must worship in spirit and in truth. (JOHN 4:20–21, 23–4)

This universal accessibility of God through Christ was described in the letter to the Hebrews, where Christ's priesthood brings a new relationship with God, freed of locality and nationhood: "But now Christ has come, high priest of good things already in being. The tent of his priesthood is a greater and more perfect one, not made by men's hands, that is, not belonging to this created world" (HEBREWS 9:11). It was as though the Cross opened the gates of Jerusalem and gave the city of God the potential to be wherever God ruled in the hearts of people. So St Paul expressed the crossing of barriers and boundaries in dramatic terms, both in terms of our freedom and in terms of Christian relationship with Jews: "There is no such thing as Jew and Greek, slave and freeman, male and female; for you are all one person in Christ Jesus" (GALATIANS 3:28), and a "single new humanity" without frontiers was initiated:

> For he is himself our peace. Gentiles and Jews, he has made the two one, and in his own body of flesh and blood has broken down the enmity which stood like a dividing wall between them; for he annulled the law with its rules and regulations, so as to create out of the two a single new humanity in himself, thereby making peace. (EPHESIANS 2:14–15)

There are serious implications here not only for Zionism, but also for nationalism, and indeed it raises uncomfortable questions about patriotism.

A journalist from the *Daily Telegraph* once interviewed me to write a personal profile. At one point in the discussion he said, "Of course the unforgivable sin you commit is a lack of patriotism." As someone who cannot bear to listen to the radio when England is losing at cricket, has a great love and admiration for the royal family, believes passionately in our Parliament, always touches down at Heathrow with great relief and can never see a really good reason for going anywhere else – I was puzzled. I couldn't get any evidence from the journalist, but the general drift seemed to be that on occasion I and my colleagues had criticized the government, had not rejoiced without reservation in the Falklands victory and had asked questions about the morality of our international investments. It is clear to me that a love of our country is a proper value and should be recognized both in our own experience and in the experience of other nations. But the service of God's Kingdom, the working towards a single new humanity in Christ, means that there are higher criteria even than my love of my country. This is not only a problem for the individual, but also for the Church. It was George Bell, Bishop of Chichester during the Second World War, who said, "The Church is not the State's spiritual auxiliary with exactly the same ends as the State . . . It has to preach the Gospel of redemption"; and he knew the cost of saying it. The love of our country must in the end be secondary to the love of our Lord. This will mean that as individuals and as the Church we shall sometimes have to question the *zeitgeist* of the nation − out of love for the nation and love for the Lord. As Dietrich Bonhoeffer demonstrated, this is not in the end a clash of interests, because out of the love of his Lord he opposed Nazism to his death, and this was the true patriotism − the true love of his nation. So, for instance, the Church's opposition to the imposition of visas for visitors from New Commonwealth countries was motivated by a love of the Lord and a love of our country. The love of our Lord called the Church to be concerned about our treatment of the alien in our midst, and the love of our country called the Church to resist the tendency to make our insitutional and national behaviour discriminate against racial minorities.

There have been so many occasions recently when nationalism in Europe has looked foolish. The Chernobyl disaster caused a cloud to pass across Europe and affect our air and our rain and our plants and livestock. Our acid rain has damaged trees in Scandinavia. Chemicals poured into the Rhine in Switzerland and flowed down to the sea, killing much of the river's life. Such disasters do not recognize national frontiers. Yet at the same time we have seen a welling-up of a longing for greater international co-operation — a desire for peace, a massive voluntary individual response to the problem of feeding the drought-ridden people of Africa. The multi-national companies stride the globe like a Colossus, but who calls them to account and helps them to use their massive influence for good? Though we see the terrifying division around us, yet there are also signs that we are beginning to understand that we are one world. The psalmist laid a curse on himself if Jerusalem was not his greatest joy, but we look for the new Jerusalem, where there will be an end to death and mourning and to crying and pain, for the old order will pass away.

As so often in the psalms, we step from the sublime to the most basic desire for vengeance:

> *Remember O Lord against the Edomites*
> *the day of Jerusalem:*
> *how they said "Down with it, down with it!*
> *raze it to its foundations."*
> *O daughter of Babylon, you that lay waste:*
> *happy shall he be who serves you as you have served us;*
> *happy shall he be who takes your little ones:*
> *and dashes them against the stones.*

The names of Edom and Babylon were both the trigger of hate and the longing for revenge. Their offence against God, their offence against God's chosen people, and their offence against Jerusalem were unforgivable. All the grief and terror of being occupied territory, of being overrun by huge armies, of seeing children killed and starved to death, poured into this desire for revenge: "Happy shall he be who takes your children and dashes them against the stones." These words are obscene, yet so much part of our human nature. Recently the Prime Minister of Israel said of Palestinians who had protested: "They will be smashed against the rocks." Rage in our world is commonplace, stalking though the lynch mob, the riot, the retaliation. It would be easier to understand it if we had seen our children torn apart by enemies, or if we had been manacled by red raw limbs to the mast. Crying for blood, for vengeance, is primeval human experience. When Cain killed Abel, the Lord said to him, "What have you done? Hark! Your brother's blood that has been shed is crying out to me from the ground" (Genesis 4:10). This primitive gut reaction is strengthened by the sense that justice demands vengeance. Severity of punishment was needed in tribal society to show that justice still reigned and would not be violated. If the revenge was not allowed, and the punishment was withheld, then it was as if the whole fabric of society would collapse, and in some way the gods would have been dethroned. It was necessary to uphold justice, and this gave added impetus to the craving for revenge. This craving had to be curbed, and the revenge allowed only to match the offence:

> When one man injures and disfigures his fellow-countryman, it shall be done to him as he has done; fracture for fracture, eye for eye, tooth for tooth; the injury and disfigurement that he has inflicted upon another shall in turn be inflicted upon him. (LEVITICUS 24:20)

It was necessary to recognize that the people of Israel were also sinners, that if God's justice was not to be violated, they too would have to be punished. God would re-establish His own righteousness.

The picture they painted of God bore the marks of the rage of those who were doing the painting. Human beings have been willing to look at the destruction of cities, the suffocation of men, women and children in the lava from a volcano, the shattering earthquake, as the signs of the vengeance of God. Man's own desire for revenge has portrayed God in our own image, and claimed the plagues and floods as appropriate weapons of God's just requirements. Yet whilst it may have been possible to see it that way in the myth, legend and experience of the past, I do not believe that in the light of Christ we can see it that way in the present. It makes you wonder why God allowed the human experiment to begin again after the flood, after Sodom and Gomorrah, after the plagues of blood and locusts. Seeing God through the reflection of Jesus makes that vengeful God seem strange. Yet Jesus himself referred to the judgement – He did not speak lightly of the mercy and forgiveness of God. People chose wicked ways and they reaped wickedness. We have to beware of our projection of our own nastiness on to God. The chief of the Manchester Police, Mr John Anderton, was quoted as saying that victims of AIDS were "wallowing in their own cess-pool." We have to consider what sort of God would subject his creatures to that sort of death, however they had behaved. We have to ask whether a victim of AIDS who repented of his sins would be healed of the illness, as the mercy of God would seem to demand, and we would also need to ask how God should be so indiscriminate that people who had committed no sin should be infected. Such punishment would

226

demonstrate the injustice of the divine administration. When I sing "Amazing grace that saved a wretch like me", I remember that such a claim not only says something about my new life, but also about the nature and character of God.

Before we feel too superior to the psalmist in his cry for vengeance, we ought to look around us in our own nation and our own community and see ourselves as we are. In the week that I am writing this chapter I have seen on the television news Young Conservatives demanding the death penalty shouting, "String them up"; the court trying young people charged with the murder of a policeman being told by the witnesses how people shouted "We've got the pig," and stabbed him many times; and the sentences issued to men who had committed rape and assault and aggravated burglary being described as too small. The tremendous sense of injustice and the craving to punish and to exact revenge remain a potent force in our lives. It is built on smaller and more personal foundations – our resentment of our parents' unfairness, when infant Cains rise up and exact revenge from their infant brothers and sisters; the estranged husbands and wives who are going to take each other "for every penny they've got"; the victims of other people's ambitions who want to turn the tables and see their oppressor humiliated. We would be totally wrong to allow ourselves to think for one moment that the desire for revenge is something that happens to other people and other ages. We dress it up in subtle guise – we speak of the necessary deterrent, the defence of decency, the rule of law and order, and no doubt there is some truth in this; but often lurking within the calm and rational response is a deep and irrational craving for revenge and punishment for their own sake. We plunge into the endless cycle of violence which is the mark of the human race — and which is not apparent, for instance, in the animal kingdom. Almost every week in Northern Ireland we hear a soldier has been shot, or a mother has been shot in the presence of her children, or a member of the police force has been shot on his return home — as reprisals.

It is in this dark pit of human experience that they chained, whipped and condemned Christ. "Crucify him! crucify him!" they cried. "His blood be on us." There is something desperate and crushing about the baying for blood. It is part of the whole truth of God and man as we see it in Christ. It is as though the whole hell of humanity in its anger and resentment cries out until it is hoarse, with its craving for vengeance. Yet Christ somehow broke the pattern, when he said, "Father, forgive them; they do not know what they are doing" (LUKE 23:34). When accused, he remained silent, when condemned, he forgave. "*Tollit peccata mundi*" — he bore the sins of the world. What he had said in his life: "Pray for your persecutors, love your enemies, turn the other cheek" — he lived out in his dying. It seems to have been the only solution of a God of love and righteousness.

> Mercy and truth are met together;
> righteousness and peace have kissed each other.
>
> (PSALM 85:10)

The incomparable justice of God, the endless cry for vengeance by man, were somehow poured through the crucible of Christ. All man's cruelty and rage were expressed, and the worst we could offer was absorbed and transformed by God — who proclaimed in His incarnate life, "Justice is mine, says the Lord, I will repay" (ROMANS 12:19).

The implications of this are staggering for us as individuals, and for us as communities and nations. Disciples of Christ, when we ponder this amazing love, wonder how on earth it can be embodied. We can imagine, perhaps, how in our individual lives we may be so changed as to carry out the commandment of Christ to love and forgive, though even that seems beyond us — but by prayer and love, perhaps we shall begin to turn the hatred upside-down and to transform our desire for revenge into a desire for healing. But when we look at communities and nations we hardly know how to begin, nor see it as practical. It may have been possible for individual Jews to forgive the Nazis, but could Israel? It may be possible for individuals to act with generosity towards those who offend against them, but can the state? My whole life has been changed by this dying of Christ for me, because I see in Him, quite unfairly, unjustly, irrationally, my many sins absorbed, suffered and carried to the grave.

Maybe it is because I cannot tolerate myself that I have found this Lord, who tolerates me, such a wonderful salvation. I have had in my life such anger at myself that I must either express it in anger against others or turn it inward on myself. Yet in seeing Christ's love for me — just as I am — and recognizing that in Him I can know that God does not abandon His holiness to forgive me, I am called to a new direction in life. It will never allow the self to be satisfied with hate or the desire for punishment and revenge, because I see that that is where I myself would stand before God if there was no Christ.

I remember that by chance I was in the BBC studios the day after the St Paul's service following the Falklands victory. The Archbishop of Canterbury had expressed the grief of war, had not seen fit to glory in victory, but had seen only people – young soldiers and their families. I was asked to comment on the fierce anger of those who said we should have given glory to God for the victory, and shouted our thanksgiving. I found myself with very few words to say, but felt the tears of the impossibility of things. I understood the glory of the victory, but in the real conflicts of the world, the defeat of others is always too present, too sharp, to allow joy much space. This is the beginning of being a stranger to the way the world thinks and why, the more we are exposed to the inner power of the Cross of Christ, we feel ourselves powerless in the world.

One of our local MPs was speaking at a meeting to ban the sale of knives in the shops in east London. The aims of the campaign were right – it grew out of the death of a young boy by stabbing. As the meeting progressed, the people began to ask for the reintroduction of the death penalty. The MP quietly and firmly tackled the issue and gave his reasons why he and other MPs continued to vote against it in the House of Commons. I thanked God for him – because I could imagine others who would play up to the crowd. In his quiet argument there was a hint of a way. He was much nearer to Christ than many a Christian who has gloried in war and conquered and tortured people – all perhaps in the name of the god of revenge and earthly victory, even when they call him Christ.

The difficulty of helping the revelation of Christ to take

shape in the world can be seen in the debate and experience of the prison service. Any practical person living in the real world will probably accept that society needs to be protected from certain forms of behaviour. It can be argued that society also needs punishment in order to maintain the order and expectations of justice and to act as a deterrent to anti-social behaviour, but the use of imprisonment to satisfy the desire for revenge is a totally different matter. I shared in an investigation of the C1 psychiatric ward in Holloway prison. We found desperately sick women there. Their mental illness was being seriously aggravated by the conditions in which they were living, and by the regime of punishment which was expected to be carried out by the prison officers. Or again, we could see the weakening of the ideal that there should be a strongly reformative element to the prison sentences which would involve education, opportunity for self-understanding, the mediation of forgiveness. Yet the regime in our prisons in London, of necessity, often has to concentrate on punishment, twenty-three-hours a day confinement, overcrowding, the denial of privacy. If people try to engage in reform, they are often labelled as soft, do-gooders, as undermining the punishing and vindictive needs of society. So the question emerges for the Christian prison officer, for the prison chaplain – "How can the forgiveness of Christ on which we depend become available to the prisoners?" If the mood of society becomes more punitive, more demanding of revenge, then how can we fight for our duty to give opportunity for reform and new life? This conflict was once symbolically expressed for me when a prison governor forbade the relatives of a woman whom I was confirming to come and share the occasion. The reason given was that the visitors would intrude on the privacy of the other prisoners at the service. My reading of the situation was that this was a clear attempt to prevent the woman being treated as a loved child of Christ, forgiven and restored, who needed her mum and dad with her on what was for her a precious occasion. As far as I can judge, prisoners have little or no privacy in prison, and most prisoners seem to be moved by the demonstration of God's love and forgiveness and special acceptance of the prisoner which being confirmed conveys.

So I can see and understand in myself and in society and in the psalmist the desire for revenge. I, who have led a protected and privileged life, in the sense that I have been much loved and secure, have to recognize that I have not tasted the desire for revenge in the same way as the father of a small child killed in Beirut or the mother of a starving child in Ethiopia — it could then be a great and overriding passion; but I am persuaded that in Christ the price has been paid for me and for them, and as we stare into that pit and look into His eyes, we begin to see that forgiveness is the means whereby God changes the world. When we read these hard verses in the psalms, we stare into the origins of rage and hate in ourselves and in the world, and bring them to our notice so that we may see the sickness and expose it to the healing love of Christ.

So this great psalm evokes the slavery in human life, and identifies the faith, the love and the hate which wrestle with each other as we make our pilgrimage to the eternal City, where we shall be finally "at home" with God. Perhaps the last word should rest with St Augustine, expressing the hope of ultimate victory:

. . . let longing for the everlasting Jerusalem grow and be strengthened in your hearts. Your captivity will pass away, your happiness will come; the last enemy will be destroyed, and we shall triumph with our King, without death.[7]

# PSALM 139
## The Intimacy of
## Almighty God

*O Lord you have searched me out and known me:*
*you know when I sit or when I stand*
*you comprehend my thoughts long before.*

*You discern my path and the places where I rest:*
*you are acquainted with all my ways.*

*For there is not a word on my tongue:*
*but you Lord know it altogether.*

*You have encompassed me behind and before:*
*and have laid your hand upon me.*

*Such knowledge is too wonderful for me:*
*so high that I cannot endure it.*

*Where shall I go from your spirit:*
*or where shall I flee from your presence?*

*If I ascend into heaven you are there:*
*if I make my bed in the grave you are there also.*

*If I spread out my wings towards the morning:*
*or dwell in the uttermost parts of the sea,*

*even there your hand shall lead me:*
*and your right hand shall hold me.*

## The Lord's Song

If I say, "Surely the darkness will cover me:
and the night will enclose me",

the darkness is no darkness with you
but the night is as clear as the day:
the darkness and the light are both alike.

For you have created my inward parts:
you knit me together in my mother's womb.

I will praise you for you are to be feared:
fearful are your acts and wonderful your works.

You knew my soul, and my bones were not hidden from you:
when I was formed in secret
and woven in the depths of the earth.

Your eyes saw my limbs when they were yet imperfect:
and in your book were all my members written;

day by day they were fashioned:
and not one was late in growing.

How deep are your thoughts to me O God:
and how great is the sum of them!

Were I to count them
they are more in number than the sand:
were I to come to the end I would still be with you.

If only you would slay the wicked O God:
if only the men of blood would depart from me!

For they affront you by their evil:
and your enemies exalt themselves against you.

*Do I not hate them O Lord that hate you:*
*do I not loathe those who rebel against you?*

*I hate them with a perfect hatred:*
*they have become my enemies.*

*Search me out O God and know my heart:*
*put me to the proof and know my thoughts.*

*Look well lest there be any way of wickedness in me:*
*and lead me in the way that is everlasting.*

There has been plenty of expert discussion about this much-loved psalm. Most scholars agree that the version in the psalter dates from a period after the exile, and that it is a meditation for use in worship. But the psalm demonstrates a contrast which we find it difficult to resolve. Verses 1–18 are a great inspired exploration of our most intimate relationship with wonderful mysterious God, and they are followed by verses 19–22 which are full of hate and conflict and a passionate call on God to use His power to destroy "the men of blood". The psalm ends with a challenge to God to test the writer to prove his innocence and a prayer that God will lead him in the right way.

In the Alternative Service Book, a discreet bracket has been placed round verses 19–22 in an attempt to draw a veil over this rather primitive outburst. Yet I want to argue that the psalm is very much a unity, and only by reading it as such shall we discover its depth and penetration.

When we go into church to pray, we go with many things on our minds. It may well be that we are feeling great anger because we ourselves have been unjustly treated, or because we are overwhelmed by the wickedness of the way people are exercising their power in the world. Most of us know the passions of resentment, of hate, and fear of the power of evil. I remember on one occasion having to face a gang of youths who were armed with staves and trying to attack another group of boys on a coach. I did not have much choice but to stand between them and persuade them to leave. When I got home afterwards I burst into tears. I have no difficulty understanding the stress and resentment and pain experienced by the beat policemen. If we live in the real world, we shall encounter violence and conflict, the misuse of power and the men of blood. For many years in east London I have found myself fighting the hate inside myself for those who do violence to our community, whether from inside or from outside. My visits to southern Africa have put our own struggles into some perspective. There I have met mothers whose small children have been detained, whose older children have been tortured. I have seen the way in which poor blacks have been used by the whites to torture and persecute other blacks. I have seen the insults and the degrading behaviour of people against their brothers and sisters because of their different colour, and felt insulted and full of anger myself. I have seen and smelt the degrading poverty of the townships and the refugee children, trudging from nation to nation in search of a home. I do not look on these things as though they were the acts of good people – but rather the result of the uncompromisingly wicked acts of the men of blood.

So, from the tame resentment and anger of my own secure life to the indignation and wrath at the wickedness of humanity to man, I know something of the desire to curse, to call down the judgement of God, to pray that wicked people will be defeated. The hate in us, especially when we are exposed to violence and injustice, is a most common experience of mankind.

But what do we do with this hate and resentment if it is not to emerge in the desire for vengeance? I can see only one way, and that is through prayer and coming to know and sense the powerful love of God. "There is no means of casting out this sort but prayer," said Jesus of the evil spirit (MARK 9:29). It is totally natural that the person who loves God, who has been plunged into hate, should go back to the Temple and try to concentrate the mind and heart on the beauty, the Almighty love of God – to put himself or herself into the hands of God, to discover that healing which will free their personality from the vice of hate. So this psalm is for me a unity. I understand and recognize the way in which these sublime thoughts about God go together in the psalmist's mind with the curse and the desire for God's punishment to be executed.

The power of the psalm comes from its personal expression of the encounter with God in the middle of the darkness of the oppression being experienced. It is not a statement of the abstract concept of God as omnipotent, omnipresent, but rather an engagement of the "I" of the person with the "Thou" of God. It is a most direct expression of that most inward conversation with the Lord God who made us.

\* \* \* \* \*

*O Lord you have searched me out and known me:*
*you know when I sit or when I stand*

*you comprehend my thoughts long before.*
*You discern my path and the places where I rest:*
*you are acquainted with all my ways.*
*For there is not a word on my tongue:*
*but you Lord know it altogether.*
*You have encompassed me behind and before:*
*and have laid your hand upon me.*
*Such knowledge is too wonderful for me:*
*so high that I cannot endure it.*

"You know me entirely Lord." There cannot be anyone who has contemplated the intimacy of God in our lives who has not felt the hint of the fear and the wonder. "You have searched me out and known me." There is a sense of nervousness and awe before God's all-seeing eye. It is not surprising that God's capacity to look right into our hearts, to search our personality like a laser, can rouse our anxiety. The accuser in our own personality, who is always ready to speak up and present us to ourselves in the worst possible light, gets confused with the search of God. Although there are many people who need to learn to say "I'm sorry", there are many others who feel bad and inadequate all the time and are endlessly pursued by their perceived need to say "I'm sorry". But the thought of being searched and known by God is in the first place enough to make anyone want to run away and hide. St Augustine likened us to the Prodigal Son, who ran away from his father. In running away, he found only bankruptcy of life and then, when all his resources were wasted, and he had nothing more, the Spirit of God spoke to him and called him back to his father. Like Adam and Eve, we suddenly know that we are naked and cannot bear the total scrutiny of God. How could He look on us without ridicule, without judgement or punishment? We know ourselves only too well. We nurse a fear that we must be unacceptable to God and thus create a distance between ourselves and God. As Isaiah said, when caught up in the vision of God in the temple: "Woe is me! I am lost, for I am a man of unclean lips and I dwell among a people of unclean lips.' (ISAIAH 6:5)

So the temptation of man is to identify the loving, searching, knowing eye of God with the accuser. This leads in our religious life and in our personal life to the constant and crippling addiction to the need to appease both God and everyone, which is a sort of violence against the self.

But the psalmist breaks through this initial anxiety at the thought of the intimate search of God into a sense of awe and wonder and thankfulness that God has this intimate knowledge. I have the picture of a small child who has done something he ought not to. "I wondered why it was so quiet in there!" – the parent comes into the room and sees a face covered with chocolate lifted from the forbidden tin. The parent is angry and the child knows he is wrong and tries to hide – but in a way dreads most of all that he will not be caught. He knows that he is secure in his parents' love and, whilst he regrets the wrath of the moment, he knows and longs for the love which it represents and expresses and which he knows of old will lead to forgiveness, acceptance and that marvellous snuggle before bedtime. The hugeness and pervading presence of God are so overwhelming that we are like a small child in His hands. Yet there is the strong sense that His main purpose is love, and so there is an enormous sense of relief that He has searched us out and known us. The Lord has found me and knows me entirely. "Oh God . . . thank God."

So I am now in the hands of God. All my life is laid out before Him. He is intimate with all my thoughts and actions – my standing, my sitting, my journeys, my words – he knows them all. He sees below the mask, the public self, into the secret places and the private world. God knows all the secrets of our heart. That thought reduces us at first to nothing. Can we bear God knowing everything about us – God seeing every action, hearing every thought? It is impossible. The most divine computer could never register – let alone assess – everyone's thoughts. Yet we have to remember that the cause of all being is intimately involved in the whole creation. As St John says of the *Logos*, "No single thing was created without him" (JOHN 1:3). We have to think of God in eternity transcending, communicating through the whole created universe. That does not seem any less credible to me than the incredible existence of the universe itself. But the all-seeing of God is not like Big Brother's eyes, or the Secret Service, committed to our repression and punishment, but to mercy and love. The mercy of God informs us that it is no good pretending, because the masks do not fool God, because He knows us entirely. "For there is not a word on my tongue but you Lord know it altogether" (v3). So, in prayer, we can give ourselves totally to God – no pretence, no self-defence, no list of achievements – just ourselves. There is a great relief in this, because so much of our life is spent trying to live up to the expectations of others, trying to live out the picture we have of ourselves, and trying to live up to the expectations of God. But we don't! So we throw ourselves on God's all-knowing, all-seeing mercy.

At this point the psalmist is overwhelmed by the wonder of the thought. The light and love of God are all around us.

> *Such knowledge is too wonderful for me*
> *so high that I cannot endure it.*

How well this translation captures the beauty of holiness. The sense of God lifts our whole being, gives us vivid clarity, a sense of sharper vision, a mingling of intense happiness, and yet at the same time is aweful, high and lifted up, like a vast mountain or the deep sea. Somehow our spirituality needs the sense of both the amazing intimacy of God and His holiness, so that our knowledge of Him is so wonderful it can hardly be endured.

\* \* \* \* \*

> *Where shall I go from your spirit:*
> *or where shall I flee from your presence?*
> *If I ascend into heaven you are there:*
> *if I make my bed in the grave you are there also.*
> *If I spread out my wings towards the morning:*
> *or dwell in the uttermost parts of the sea,*
> *even there your hand shall lead me:*
> *and your right hand shall hold me.*

The knowledge that is too high to be endured leads straight back to the desire to flee. In many of us there is an urge to escape from God. We can see it in the way people (perhaps especially men) try to crush the intimations of God they are given. It is often especially true of those whom God calls for a specific purpose. Moses, Jeremiah and Jonah all wanted to hide from the presence and calling of God. But there is no escape from the Spirit of God, in heaven or earth or under the earth, in the widest limits of the universe. As St Augustine asked, "Who can in the world flee from that Spirit, with Whom the world is filled? . . . Where is God not?"[1] As is so characteristic of this psalm, the awesome fact of the inescapability of God is turned into a source of supreme comfort. The pervasive God will hold us and lead us wherever our destiny shall take us. The fact that we cannot escape brings an assurance that God will never let us go – never let us down or fail us – wherever we have to go, whatever may be our struggles: "Even there your hand shall lead me, and your right hand shall hold me."

This assurance reminds me of St Paul's affirmation in the letter to the Romans:

> For I am convinced that there is nothing in death or life, in the realm of spirits or superhuman powers, in the world as it is or the world as it shall be, in the forces of the universe, in heights or depths – nothing in all creation that can separate us from the love of God in Christ Jesus our Lord. (ROMANS 8:38–9)

Whether it was the turmoil of the natural world or the terrors of the supernatural, nothing could separate him from the love of God in Christ Jesus. This vision is of great importance. We often think of areas of our life and experience as being out of reach of God – God-forsaken. The places where we are humiliated, defeated and depressed can seem empty of God or unreachable by His love.

I remember someone saying of my parish, "Not that God-forsaken place!" How many times, too, have I heard people express the view that people of other races are God-forsaken people. Also, I have sometimes encountered in myself the sense that God cannot reach into my heart enough to change me, and that some of my behaviour is God-forsaken. This is especially true of my sins, when I shut the door on God by my own deliberate actions, perhaps even recognizing precisely what I am doing as I do it. But I have come to believe that not only am I not God-forsaken, not only are places and people not God-forsaken, but even that God is sometimes especially close in that experience of forsakenness. This is difficult to take, as indeed Isaiah found in his vision of the one who was to save Israel:

> He grew up before the Lord like a young plant
>   whose roots are in parched ground:
> he had no beauty, no majesty to draw our eyes,
>   no grace to make us delight in him;
> his form, disfigured, lost all the likeness of a man.
>   his beauty changed beyond human semblance.
> He was despised, he shrank from the sight of men,
>   tormented and humbled by suffering;
>   we despised him, we held him of no account,
>   a thing from which men turn away their eyes.
>
> (ISAIAH 53:2–3)

No person, no place, no people is beyond the reach of God and His redemption – they may even be going through the necessary gate by which a way is opened for them. Our battles with our own personality, with temptation, may be part of a process which saves others. Even when we fall and know the sense of separation from God, and try to stand again in the light of the love of God, we are part of the universal search for God, the striving to overcome the power of evil with the power of forgiveness and love. ". . . there will be greater joy in heaven over one sinner who repents than over ninety-nine righteous people who do not need to repent." (LUKE 15:7)

"If I make my bed in the grave, you are there also" (v7). Even in the ultimate place of death, where the body is inert and the brain stopped, even there God is not reduced to nothing, but raises me from death. There is nowhere where you are not, Lord.

\* \* \* \* \*

> If I say, "Surely the darkness will cover me:
> and the night will enclose me",
> the darkness is no darkness with you
> but the night is as clear as the day:
> the darkness and the light are both alike.

As a boy, I was desperately afraid of the dark. I remember imagining burglars coming in through the ventilator in my room. I was terrified of being caught in a lane behind our house in the dark, and remember running home panic-stricken as the brambles clawed at me. I can still relive the fear of being trapped in an old air raid shelter. I have had adult experiences which have replayed those old tapes in my mind, when the uncanny sense of being pursued or trapped has made my heart thump and made me walk quietly, pretending not to run towards the light. I remember walking back home through the concrete corridors of Thamesmead late at night and sensing some threat. I think also of the nightmares I have had, when the dream slips into waking and I am sure there is someone standing over my bed. I will never forget my dear old Dad crashing into my room at night as he had his stroke, and my waking/sleeping terror. I know a little of the fear of darkness and I know from children and others how great it can be. "Surely the darkness will cover me and the night will enclose me." But the psalmist is not just talking about the darkness of the night, but also about what the darkness symbolizes — the darkness of the soul and the threat to our peace, the dread of descending into Sheol, the place of dark shades, where we lose our grip on life in the darkness of death.

The two greatest sources of darkness in my life — that is in my inward life — have been grief and shame. They both involve a sense of loss of ourselves, the first through loss of someone or something dear to us, and the second through the loss of our sense of self-respect. Susan Hill, in her book *The Springtime of the Year*, describes the descent into darkness of spirit which bereavement can bring. It is as though someone has cut away that part of our brain and our feelings which provided us with light and hope. As though we are crushed and compressed so that our waking hours are occupied by invading hurt from which we bleed inwardly. It is as though our heads are bent down and we do not know how to lift them, and tears are beyond us. It is an experience of darkness in the sense that we become desperately self-contained, as though for a time no one or nothing can reach into us and lighten our will. So we go through the motions of social behaviour, but really we are in a sort of death ourselves. The hard thing about this grief is not only that it threatens to cover us, overwhelm us, drown us, but it joins up with all the other lesser griefs we have known and fear might be.

The darkness of shame brings a different pain because it is self-inflicted. It involves the shattering of the best image we have of ourselves. It is recognizable as an expression which begins very early in our lives when other children mock us or humiliate us, or when we feel despicable in the eyes of adults. It deepens in the discoveries and experiences of adolescence and is full grown in the mature judgement of our own wrong-doing. It is an area of our lives where illness can be conceived, where an exaggerated sense of guilt or a deadened amorality can emerge. But it is part of our maturing process, when we experience the darkness of shame at the wrong we do. It is a dangerous emotion, and sometimes we need the perspective of another person to reflect whether we are experiencing the healthy darkness of proper shame or the unhealthy darkness of a distorted or distorting personality.

St Augustine seems to have been a person who was much afflicted by wicked thoughts. As I read his exposition, I became aware of the great personal battle being fought all the time in himself. It was as though his special soul was especially tempted, especially subject to the darts of the evil one. This meant that he descended into the hell of the struggle, and therefore knew every twist and trick the evil impulse uses in us. For some, he will prove to be a much-needed friend on the journey, who knows and recognizes the snares and traps, but for others who are not so afflicted, he will seem too caught up with evil, with lust, with those things which drag man down. For him, I guess, Babylon was like the great teeming night-life of the city, threatening to engulf the runaway. He must have experienced captivity there and known the longing, the tearing apart he describes, the desire for the everlasting city of light: "For lust was the lime of our wings, it dashed us down from the freedom of the sky, that is, the free breezes of the Spirit of God."[2] But he drew comfort from the fact that he was discomforted, that he knew such self-accusation, because it was a sign that God cared for him and was calling him back, by his discontent. Like the Prodigal, the runaway would rise up and go to his father. He gave practical advice as to how to battle against the evil: "When lust is born, before evil habit giveth it strength against thee, when lust is little, by no means let it gain the strength of evil habit; when it is little, dash it . . . 'Dash it against the Rock; and that Rock is Christ' (1 CORINTHIANS 10:4)."[3]

Augustine warned against self-justification. The most important path to health was recognition of the darkness in ourselves. ". . . by defending thy darkness, thou shalt darken thy darkness."[4] As he says again and again, it is we ourselves who make space for the wickedness in our lives, and the only way to counter its power is to fill our lives with the love of God: "Thou art full of evil desires; if I tell of those good things of Jerusalem, thou takest them not in; thou must be emptied of that wherewith thou art full, that thou mayest be filled with that whereof thou art empty."[5] Yet in all this he is aware of the need of God: "We have free-will; but even with that free-will what can we do, unless He help us Who commandeth us?"[6]

But there is another meaning in this verse which seems more appropriate to its setting, where the darkness is seen as a place to hide in, and especially as a place to hide, in order to escape from the judgement of God. Just as we often behave differently if someone is watching us than if we think we are in private, so the psalmist for a moment imagines that God cannot see him in the dark. The candid camera embarrasses its victims by showing to the public what they were doing privately. It is one of the great gains of world-wide media, that the private atrocities of nations become public property and therefore accountable to the public conscience and condemnation. The shameful deeds of torture, brutality and fraud done in the darkness are brought out into the open – exposed to the judgement. It is a common expression that "the only sin is being found out". The psalmist is clear that whilst we may be able to conceal our crimes from other people or from the public gaze, we cannot hide them from the all-seeing gaze of God.

Whether we take the first meaning of the overwhelming experiences of darkness in our lives, or the second meaning, that we can hide in the darkness from the all-seeing God, verse 11 counters our fear by reminding us that God transcends the earthly darkness with His glorious light. "The darkness is no darkness . . . darkness and light are both alike." From the beginning of Genesis to the closing chapter of the Book of Revelation, the Bible is full of light. "God said, 'Let there be light,' and there was light." Genesis 1:3 describes the primeval dawn, and the Book of Revelation describes the eternal light of the city of God: "There shall be no more night, nor will they need the light of lamps or sun, for the Lord God will give them light; and they shall reign for evermore" (REVELATION 22:5). Throughout the text, the light keeps on breaking through and shining, both to bring joy and well-being and also to show up the dark and hidden corners of the soul. Those who read the Bible regularly will have received so many pictures of the Light of God – the radiant face of Moses reflecting the light and glory of God; the vision of the servant of God in Isaiah as the bringer of light (Isaiah 42); the star of Bethlehem and the light of the angels; the claim of Christ that He is the Light of the World; the conversion of St Paul in the blinding light of the encounter with Christ on the Damascus Road; and finally the light of the eternal City – the light which shines in everyone and which cannot be extinguished.

There is therefore no conceivable chance of hiding in the darkness from God, any more than Adam and Eve could hide in the garden of Eden. God sees and knows every hidden secret of our lives: "For he will bring to light what darkness hides, and disclose men's inward motives" (1 CORINTHIANS 4:5). God sees and knows us ultimately – that is, before our beginning and after our ending. God sees what we are and what we do with our whole lives – just as He sees what everyone does with their whole lives. This is an impossible idea to comprehend. I am bewildered at seeing an underground train full of people, or flying over a city, trying to imagine all those flats and houses and rooms with all their people. Yet the fact that they exist at all, that they have brains and destinies and loves and sorrows – that is also an incomprehensible miracle. We flounder when we try to move from our own little narrow perspective to the perspective of universality and eternity. God is beyond our thoughts, and yet His light is in every being and cannot be extinguished.

Again this threat of the all-seeing eye of God becomes a source of comfort. It is not like Big Brother, but the eye of love — like the eyes of Christ on Peter as the cock crew, on the people as they demanded His life — like the eyes of Christ on the child whose innocence reflected the Kingdom of God. It is a comfort because we are known and seen. We may have secrets, we may carry a burden of shame, we may feel defeated, but God sees and tells us to look up to Him and our face will shine. There is light all around us, and we are seen and forgiven and alight when we turn to Him. There is a marvellous power in the vision that we are known, and seen, and accepted, and forgiven, and called. In heaven we shall know as we are known — we shall see as we are seen.

I suppose I should not be surprised that someone who was afraid of the dark should have first discovered the glimmering of the light of God in the dark. My own first recognized encounter with God was on Christmas night. My friends wanted me to go to midnight Mass, but I would not go into the church because we were rather drunk — though I thought I was an unbeliever. I sat outside in the dark and sobered up sitting on a very cold tombstone beneath a majestic starry sky. I could hear my friends' raucous singing above the more tuneful rendering of the congregation. Yet in the darkness I began to see that my life was upside-down and that there was no darkness equal to trying to live without God. I did not see light, but experienced it reaching within me. Nearly all my experiences of God have been, in a way, like the light — a dawning — an unveiling — a new seeing — a revealing. I began to learn that the fear of the dark which had begun as a natural infantile response had become a symbol of my sense of guilt — the nightmare side of myself — and a lot of the fear disappeared when I realized that I was loved and accepted by God and so the threat was removed. Often now the dark is the time when I feel especially close to God: "The darkness is no darkness with you but the night is as clear as the day". St Augustine captured the profound sense of Christ invading and defeating the darkness:

> The night was made to me light, because in the night I despaired of being able to cross so great a sea, to surmount so long a journey, to reach the utmost parts by persevering to the end. Thanks to Him who sought me when a runaway . . . Christ came down into the night. Christ took flesh in this world and enlightened for us the night.[7]

In terms of the light in the darkness of grief, slow shafts of light appear, breaking it up — perhaps a new sense of God's purpose, or a new depth in a friendship, or the light of some accurate comforting words. I was standing at the altar celebrating the Eucharist as I had a thousand times before, and as I said the phrase we always use, "the whole company of heaven", it opened a gate for me to see that my mother and father had taken on a greater, freer reality, and now those words are full of light for me. There have been many other texts which have done just the same. The journey back from grief is like a sunrise in slow motion, with just a hint of light, and then light on the edges of the clouds, then the dawn, though the shadows remain.

As for the darkness of shame, the light of Christ restores our identity. We experience loss of face, or we sense that we have defaced the image of God in ourselves. It is a self-inflicted wound. We don't deserve healing, but we get it:

"For the grace of God has dawned upon the world with healing for all mankind' (TITUS 2:11). The accusation which we know to be true is set aside. Just as the smile of encouragement from another person can lift us, so there is the light in the face of God shining upon us. Our darkness will seem so small in the light of God. The night of our lives can neither hide us nor overwhelm us.

\* \* \* \*

*For you have created my inward parts:*
*you knit me together in my mother's womb.*
*I will praise you for you are to be feared:*
*fearful are your acts and wonderful your works.*
*You knew my soul and my bones were not hidden from you:*
*when I was formed in secret*
*and woven in the depths of the earth.*
*Your eyes saw my limbs when they were yet imperfect:*
*and in your book were all my members written;*
*day by day they were fashioned:*
*and not one was late in growing.*

The sentence never fails to stop me in my tracks: "You knit me together in my mother's womb." I see those miraculous photographs of the foetus slowly forming itself, becoming a recognizable shape, achieving humanity. I think of the minute premature babies in the incubators and see the brilliance of their limbs and organs. "You knit me together in my mother's womb." It is the claim of the profound intimacy of God with the creation. God is an energy involved in that growth and development of a person — of me, of you.

It is no use being starry-eyed, however, because there are viruses and miscarriages, deformities and handicaps, as the process is subject to all the possibilities and risks of coming to be. Yet in the creation process, God is the elemental source of life. When we extend the creed which says that "God knit me together in the womb", we say that God grew me as a child. God was intimately concerned in my journey to adulthood, God is intimately concerned in me now – in you now. There is a destiny, a calling. The word of the Lord came to Jeremiah: "Before I formed you in the womb I knew you for my own; before you were born I consecrated you" (JEREMIAH 1:5). There is a sense of awe, of possibility, of mystery in this thought that leads me to pause and just be open to that intimacy of God. That is what the psalmist does:

> *I will praise you for you are to be feared:*
> *fearful are your acts and wonderful your works.*

This takes us to the heart of religion. This conviction that God and man are intimately related, so that our body, our being, is filled with the Spirit of God, dependent upon the creative activity of God, and, above all, open to the creative love of God. This is where the believer and the unbeliever part, at this fundamental moment of recognizing the "Thou" in our lives, the great Being from whom we all derive. It moves us to the act of praise and wonder, lifting us for a moment from self-containment and egocentricity into loving God.

In verse 14, the only new idea is the link made between the creation of the human being and the earth:

*You knew my soul, and my bones were not hidden*
  *from you:*
*when I was formed in secret*
*and woven in the depths of the earth.*

The second Creation story says that "the Lord God formed a man from the dust of the ground and breathed into his nostrils the breath of life. Thus the man became a living creature" (GENESIS 2:7), and Psalm 103 uses the same idea:

For he knows of what we are made:
  he remembers that we are but dust.

(PSALM 103:14)

There was a wholesome recognition that we are part of the natural order — dust to dust — or as Psalm 103 also says:

The days of man are but as grass:
  he flourishes like a flower of the field;
  when the wind goes over it is gone:
  and its place will know it no more.

This idea seems to threaten our individuality and our eternal destiny. We are but dust . . . But the mythology portrayed man as being formed in the depths of mother earth. This might seem to be an impersonal existence, but it was made personal by the all-embracing love of God. Even when we were dust the Lord knew us and identified us, and this line of thought carries us into verse 15 of Psalm 139:

*Your eyes saw my limbs when they were yet imperfect:*
*and in your book were all my members written.*

God saw the formation of my body — God was intimately involved in the process, and indeed a record was kept in the record books of God. In this case, it is not referring to the Book of Judgement, but instead reminds us that God knows everything about us from first to last – rather like the sentiment of Jesus that even the hairs of our head are numbered.

\* \* \* \* \*

*How deep are your thoughts to me O God:*
*and how great is the sum of them!*
*Were I to count them*
*they are more in number than the sand:*
*were I to come to the end I would still be with you.*

"How deep are your thoughts to me O God". The psalmist has contemplated God and the mystery of his own life and come to recognize that his mind cannot grasp it all. God is truly beyond him. He declares the unsearchability of God, the unknowability of all His thoughts. Whether we are contemplating the Milky Way or the acorn or the octopus, God is ultimately beyond our finite minds. To look down a microscope or to study distant galaxies, to be absorbed in the first rays of the sun rolling the mist back from the valley, is to experience our smallness, and our ignorance. To meditate upon the responsibility of God for the world and the universe is to feel like an insect. To try to grasp the evolution of being through time and space is to be dumbfounded – and yet when all that has been said, we are precious and beloved.

Yet you have made (man) little less than a god:
and have crowned him with glory and honour.

(PSALM 8:6)

257

We can know God in the same way a man can see a limitless ocean when he is standing by the shore with a candle during the night. Do you think he can see very much? Nothing much, scarcely anything. And yet, he can see the water well, he knows that in front of him is the ocean, and that this ocean is enormous and that he cannot contain it all in his gaze. So it is with our knowledge of God.[8]

There is a temptation for the theologian to escape into the unknowability of God – in one sense it puts Him beyond argument and it certainly seems that some Christians use the mystery of God to excuse their own reluctance to use their minds. There is the word of God, often repeated, that "His ways are not our ways, His thoughts are not our thoughts." Yet at the same time the psalmist has just revelled in the fact that God was intimately involved in the creation of the human being, including his brain. So we can believe that God wishes us to use our minds. We recognize that they take us only to the foothills of God's reality, and that all our definitions, our descriptions of God, are like a child's drawing of the sea compared with the ocean's majesty. God is beyond us and beyond our reason, and we have to accept the limitations of our theology, yet Job came to the awe and the wonder through the process of using his mind and his sense of justice. Even if in prayer we end up saying, "I'm sorry, I didn't understand – you are so much more amazing than I thought," we have accepted the challenge of our human condition and offered only the best we have to God.

\* \* \* \* \*

*If only you would slay the wicked O God:*
*if only the men of blood would depart from me!*
*For they affront you by their evil:*
*and your enemies exalt themselves against you.*
*Do I not hate them O Lord that hate you:*
*do I not loathe those who rebel against you?*
*I hate them with a perfect hatred:*
*they have become my enemies.*

As I said in my introduction to this psalm, there can be few more shocking examples of the switch from the sublime to the hateful than the transition from verse 18 to verse 19. But even if these lines have been added to an original psalm ending at verse 18, it is still significant that the religious mind can make the plunge and see no inconsistency. In a way this sort of total change of mood and gear and theology is just what we all do. If we did not fall from the grace and vision of worship into the nastiness, violence and banality of everyday life, our troubles would be over. We know – because it is easier to see in others – that people are quite capable of going to church, being caught up in the prayers, the praise and communion with God, and then walking out of church and slaying their fellows with weapons or words. Religion and hate often go hand in hand, to the near despair of Christ. His attacks upon the Pharisees were the most harsh and strident because they were able to wear the religious veneer over the death and cunning of their own ambition and greed. It does not take more than a moment for the reflection of the light of God to be darkened by our own enmity. I have to admit that I can travel from the sublime to the hateful in a few short minutes, and I can especially recognize the hate described by the psalmist. I experienced hate when I saw the South African armoured cars rounding up Namibian villagers. I have experienced hate of those who exercise power in a racist way. I have hated when I saw the townships, and the starving children with flies in their nostrils. I have experienced hate of those who have publicly abused me. When seeing a young lad die of drug addiction, I have felt hate for the pushers. I have hated the lies told in the press about my friends and myself. I have been able to live with the juxtaposition of my prayers and my hate. My difference from the psalmist is that I am ashamed of my hate and want to be free of it − whereas he believes he is innocent and he is dissociating himself from those who are opposed to God. C.S. Lewis says that this is not "holier than thou", but it is just good sense to distance ourselves from the enemies of God. There is so much evil, so many "men of blood". The napalm was dropped by human beings, the concentration camps were run by human beings, children are abused and beaten by human beings. Are we all dragged into complicity? Our standard of living appears in part to depend upon the sale of arms, the denuding of poor nations' mineral resources − we all share in the guilt of the great corporations. It is understandable that we should want to free ourselves of our guilt-by-association. There are communities who try to create a clean air space around themselves where they will not be compromised and stained by sharing in the great wickedness of the world. We know something of the desire to curse, to call down the judgement of God, to pray that the wicked will be defeated and destroyed. But we ourselves are not innocent. We are all caught up in the compromises and stains, and it is in that world that we have to live out our faith. We are all under judgement, and our own hate is under the gaze and assessment of God.

Yet in the midst of all the complexities and compromises we may not abandon the moral struggle, because evil does have to be resisted. The fact that we all have sinned does not excuse our sin. The Christian life, like the Jewish life, is depicted as a battle against evil:

> Finally then, find your strength in the Lord, in his mighty power. Put on all the armour which God provides, so that you may be able to stand firm against the devices of the devil. For our fight is not against human foes, but against cosmic powers, against the authorities and potentates of this dark world, against the superhuman forces of evil in the heavens. (EPHESIANS 6:10–12)

I do not think that St Augustine's explanation of these "hating" verses will do. He makes that distinction, which today is often made, of hating the sin but not the sinner. But this passage is about down-to-earth hate – violent desires against enemies – our own and God's. Although his explanation does not fit the meaning or the text, it raises an important question: "This it is to hate with a perfect hatred, that neither on account of the vices thou hate the men, nor on account of the men love the vices."[9] Or again, he expresses his love for the sinner and hate of the sin like this: "I hated in them their iniquities, I loved Thy creation."[10]

There is a comfort and a failing in this idea. The comfort is that we are encouraged to believe that sins have almost a separate existence from us who commit them. As St Paul said, ". . . it is no longer I who perform the action, but sin that lodges in me . . . it is no longer I who am the agent" (ROMANS 7: 17,20). There are times when we feel "taken over" by bad energies, which seem to operate through us in spite of ourselves. The soul within us somewhere can objectify what has been done and reject it or repent of it. We may hope of God that He will hate that in us which is wicked, and love us that we are human.

The idea fails for two reasons. The first is that it could encourage a split in our inmost being that absolves us of responsibility for our actions, so that we could blame a sort of possession, or blame this objective energy which "made" us do it against our will. Yet there is only one way of tackling the brute fact, and that is to recognize that we ourselves, the person we are, did the wrong. Secondly, it is possible to speak about another person as though we can condemn their sin without condemning them. But we ourselves do not receive condemnation in that way. We do not say "Oh good, he's only condemning my sins, he's not condemning me," we rightly understand him to be condemning those who do the sin.

It is not possible to separate the sin from the sinner because each action we do is the result of that complex being we have become. The father of starving children sins when, in despair, he steals a loaf from his wealthy neighbour, but it is a different stealing from the wealthy neighbour stealing from the starving to add to his wealth. The prostitute who finds a love that lasts to save her, sins when she commits adultery with her lover, yet her adultery is different from that of one who has every blessing in human relationships and yet betrays his wife and children. We are responsible for our own sins, but our responsibility is seen by God in the context of our own history. God knows who we have been and who we are, He knows our river back to its source, and He alone can judge truly.

We are required to struggle against the enemies of God in His world, and against that same enemy in ourselves. Our struggle against injustice is an extension of the struggle against the same distortion of the love of God within ourselves. This, I believe, gives the context in which these hard words in verses 19–22 should be read, yet at the same time realizing that none of us is without fault.

Then the psalmist suddenly sees the implications of his hate — it is almost as though he catches himself in his self-righteousness. So he finishes with the prayer that God will test him and search him out and know him thoroughly, that he may be preserved from wickedness which he has been so ready to condemn in others. So he ends in a plea for the guidance of God:

> *Search me out O God and know my heart:*
> *put me to the proof and know my thought.*
> *Look well lest there be any way of wickedness in me:*
> *and lead me in the way that is everlasting.*

# BIBLIOGRAPHY

The Alternative Service Book 1980, Oxford University Press and
A.R. Mowbray, 1980

Anderson, A.A., *Psalms* (2 vols), The New Century Bible, Marshall,
Morgan and Scott, 1972

Augustine, Saint, *Expositions on the Book of the Psalms* (6 vols),
Oxford, John Henry Parker; London, F. & J. Rivington, 1857

The Cambridge Bible Commentary, *Psalms* (2 vols), Cambridge
University Press, 1977

Camus, Albert, *The Outsider*, Penguin

Cox, Harvey, *The Secular City*, Penguin

*Faith in the City*, Church House Publishing, 1985

Harvey, Anthony (ed.), *Theology in the City*, SPCK, 1989

Holloway, Richard, *The Sidelong Glance*, Darton, Longman and
Todd, 1985

Lewis, C.S., *Reflections on the Psalms*, Fount Paperbacks, 1977

Muilenburg, James, *The Way of Israel*, Harper and Row, 1961

Muir, Edwin, *Collected Poems*, Faber and Faber, 1960

*The New English Bible*, Oxford University Press and Cambridge
University Press, 1961, 1970

Sartre, Jean-Paul, *Nausea*, Penguin Modern Classics, 1965

Stallworthy, Jon, *Root and Branch*, Chatto and Windus and The
Hogarth Press, 1969

Weiser, Arthur, *The Psalms* (2 vols), SCM Press, 1962

# NOTES

## INTRODUCTION

1 Augustine, *Expositions on the Book of the Psalms*, vol II, p.127
2 ibid., vol. VI, p.208
3 ibid., vol. II, p.199
4 James Muilenburg, *The Way of Isr el*, p.127

## PSALM 1

1 C.S. Lewis, *Reflections on the Psalms*, pp.15–16
2 *Alternative Service Book*, p.230

## PSALM 23

1 Jon Stallworthy, *Root and Branch*
2 Quoted in Gordon Rupp, *The Righteousness of God*, pp.354–5

## PSALM 42/43

1 Augustine, op. cit., vol. II, p.182
2 ibid., vol. II, p.186
3 ibid., vol. II, p.187
4 Arthur Weiser, *The Psalms*, p.346
5 Augustine, op. cit., vol. II, p.189
6 ibid., vol. II, p.189
7 ibid., vol. II, p.192
8 ibid., vol. II, p.191
9 ibid., vol. II, p.201

10  ibid., vol. II, p.201
11  ibid., vol. II, p.197
12  ibid., vol. II, p.206


## PSALM 46

1  Haddon Wilmer, in Anthony Harvey (ed.), *Faith in the City*, Church House Publishing
2  Harvey Cox, *The Secular City*, Penguin


## PSALM 51

1  Edwin Muir, *Collected Poems*, pp.198–9
2  Augustine, op. cit., vol. II, p.378
3  ibid., vol. II, p.371
4  ibid., vol. II, p.369
5  ibid., vol. II, p.370
6  ibid., vol. II. p.371
7  A.A. Anderson, *Psalms*, p.397
8  Augustine, op. cit., vol. II, p.377
9  BBC Radio 2, "Good Morning Sunday", 6th December 1987
10  Augustine, op. cit., vol. II, p.372
11  ibid., vol. II, p.380
12  *Alternative Service Book*, p.256


## PSALM 90

1  Arthur Weiser, *The Psalms*


## PSALM 137

1  Sigmund Mowinckel, *Psalms in Israel's Worship*, Blackwell
2  Anderson, op. cit., p.897

3 Albert Camus, *The Outsider*
4 Jean-Paul Satre, *Nausea*
5 *Faith in the City*, p.xiv
6 Augustine, op. cit., vol. VI, p.158
7 ibid., vol. VI, p.177

PSALM 139

1 Augustine, op. cit., vol. VI, pp.200–1
2 ibid., vol. VI, p.202
3 ibid., vol. VI, p.176
4 ibid., vol. VI, p.204
5 ibid., vol. VI, p.167
6 ibid., vol. VI, p.203
7 ibid., vol. VI, p.203
8 Richard Holloway, *The Sidelong Glance*, pp.22–3
9 Augustine, op. cit., vol. VI, p.216
10 ibid., vol. VI, p.216

# Fount Paperbacks

Fount is one of the leading paperback publishers of religious books and below are some of its recent titles.

- ☐ PAUL THE INTERPRETER  George Appleton  £2.95
- ☐ ACTING AS FRIENDS  Michael De-la-Noy  £4.50
- ☐ THE BURNING BUSH  John Drury  £2.99
- ☐ A KEY TO THE OLD TESTAMENT
                                        David Edwards  £3.50
- ☐ THE CRY OF THE SPIRIT  Tatiana Goricheva  £3.99
- ☐ CROSSFIRE  Richard Holloway  £3.50
- ☐ CREATION  Martin Israel  £2.99
- ☐ BEING IN LOVE  William Johnston  £3.50
- ☐ THE MASS  J. M. Lustiger  £2.99
- ☐ CALLED TO HOLINESS  Ralph Martin  £2.95
- ☐ THE HIDDEN JOURNEY  Melvyn Matthews  £3.50
- ☐ REFLECTIONS ON MY WORK  Thomas Merton  £3.99
- ☐ DEATH BE NOT PROUD  Peter Mullen  £2.99
- ☐ SCRIPTURE PROMISES  Carmen Rojas  £3.50
- ☐ LIGHT AND LIFE  Grazyna Sikorska  £2.95
- ☐ EASTER GARDEN  Nicola Slee  £3.95
- ☐ CHRISTMAS – AND ALWAYS  Rita Snowden  £2.99
- ☐ CELEBRATION  Margaret Spufford  £2.95

All Fount Paperbacks are available at your bookshop or newsagent, or they can be ordered by post from Fount Paperbacks, Cash Sales Department, G.P.O. Box 29, Douglas, Isle of Man. Please send purchase price plus 22p per book, maximum postage £3. Customers outside the UK send purchase price, plus 22p per book. Cheque, postal order or money order. No currency.

NAME (Block letters) _____

ADDRESS_____

_____

_____